HOLD ONTO YOUR NAME

*The Story of
Liam 'Billy' Whelan, A Busby Babe*

by Roy Cavanagh MBE

Contents

	Acknowledgements	iii
	Introduction	v
Chapter One	In at the Deep End	1
Chapter Two	So This is Manchester	6
Chapter Three	First Team Debut	10
Chapter Four	Double Championships for Billy	14
Chapter Five	The World is your Oyster	21
Chapter Six	1957/58 Part One	33
Chapter Seven	1957/58 Part Two	38
Chapter Eight	1957/58 Part Three	43
Chapter Nine	Just who was Liam 'Billy' Whelan	47

Acknowledgements

My personal thanks to the following

Ian R Carr
and
Phil Neill
without whose help – No Book!!

Alan Bradshaw
whose idea this book was
and who kept reminding me to write it

To My Family
Barbara, Duncan, Martin, Claire, Sam,
Evie, Aila, Harvey, Jean, Jayne, Jonny and Lauren

Introduction

When a young Dubliner called Liam Whelan arrived at Old Trafford, home of Manchester United in May 1953, one of that club's greatest ever players, captains and also a fellow Dubliner, John Carey gave him a bit of advice about Mancunians. 'Whatever you do Liam, don't let them alter your name. They have called me Jackie and Johnny when it is John!' Well, William Augustine Whelan, who already had been called Liam back home, did not have much choice as the Manchester public quickly had him known as Billy as they took him to their hearts. Actually, the meeting of the two Dubliner's was to see them going different ways, as Johnny Carey was about to end his long, illustrious Manchester United playing career and embark on a managerial one, starting at Blackburn Rovers, whilst young Billy was about to start his Manchester United career.

Manchester United and Ireland has had very strong links, not just do fans regularly cross the Irish Sea to watch their favourites play at 'The Theatre of Dreams', but many men of the green nation's, either side of the borders, have gone straight onto stardom for the club as players. None, in my opinion, have surpassed the legend of Johnny Carey, but many have become such massive legends themselves, like Harry Gregg, Jackie Blanchflower, George Best, Sammy McIlroy and Norman Whiteside from the North, whilst Tony Dunne, Noel Cantwell, Kevin Moran, Frank Stapleton, Paul McGrath, Denis Irwin and Roy Keane have secured their places in the club's folklore as they followed Johnny Carey from the South of Ireland.

Billy Whelan was another, having followed Carey from the South of Ireland, indeed the same Home Farm club, he would go on at Manchester United to win two League Championships, two Charity Shield's, the FA Youth Cup, the Blue Star 'mini' World Cup, the Central League, the Manchester League as well as playing in an FA Cup Final, a European Cup semi-final, represent his country four times and be an original member of the side that was heralded as the Busby Babes. All this in five years before he was cruelly cut down with a further seven of his team mates at the end of the snowy, ice ridden Munich airport runway as Manchester United were returning from Belgrade where twenty four hours earlier they had secured their place in a second successive semi-final of the European Cup after defeating Red Star.

He was one of those special footballers whose brain moves quicker than their legs. He was marvellously agile for a man over 6ft tall, caressing a football, lethal in the opposition penalty area but able to glide over the turf, beating players with ease with his dribbling skills. Sadly, Liam 'Billy' Whelan just never realised himself how good he actually was.

A short, glorious life is now reflected back in 'Hold onto your Name'.

Chapter One
In at the Deep End

May 1953
4th May MANCHESTER UNITED v WOLVERHAMPTON WANDERERS
1st leg FA Youth Cup Final

On their way to appearing in the first ever FA Youth Cup Final, Manchester United had kept a very settled side, which was then thrown into confusion as the first leg loomed due to a knee injury to inside right John Doherty. John was a very fine player who would later win a league title for Manchester United before going onto play for Leicester City, later returning to Manchester United to organise the successful old players association. United assistant manager Jimmy Murphy, who devoted his life to making young players into complete footballers, desperately wanted to make sure Manchester United became the first winners of this prestigious new competition, particularly as Wolverhampton Wanderers would be their opponents and he was aware they also were building their future with a youth policy.

Jimmy Murphy got in touch with Manchester United's Ireland scout, Billy Behan, a man himself who had played one game for Manchester United as a goalkeeper in the mid 1930's, to ask about the talent they had been discussing. Billy had gone onto play for Shelbourne and Shamrock Rovers after leaving Manchester United before Matt Busby asked him to scout in the South of the country for them. A player United had interest in was Vinnie Ryan, a decent inside forward who decided he wanted to play for Glasgow Celtic, but Billy Behan had spotted a team mate of Vinnie's at Home Farm and had already alerted Bert Whalley, Murphy's right hand man, at United of his ability. That player was Liam 'Billy' Whelan. Billy had been with Home Farm since he was twelve playing through their age groups, indeed, at higher ones than for his age such was his ability.

So, Billy Behan was sent to see Billy at his Cabra home North of Dublin, a month after his eighteenth birthday and he was quickly over to England and to Manchester United. Billy's older brother Christy was only surprised that it had taken Manchester United so long as Billy had represented Ireland at Schoolboy's, beating England 8-4 in one match, and Youth Internationals with five of that side already signed up in England, including full back Paddy Kennedy at Manchester United. Christy also said to Billy Behan that Billy Whelan was not going to Old Trafford for a trial, only to sign on full time. Billy Behan quickly reassured Christy that it was no trial, Billy Whelan was the player Manchester United wanted.

The first leg FA Youth Cup Final tie at Old Trafford was only forty eight hours after the wonderful 1953 FA Cup Final which became immortalised as the Stanley Matthews final, despite the fact that his fellow Blackpool forward Stan Mortensen had scored a hat trick to retrieve a 1-3 deficit against Bolton Wanderers into a 4-3 triumph. With the whole country still talking about the game, Manchester was about to witness the debut of Billy Whelan alongside such as Eddie Colman, David Pegg, Eddie Lewis, Albert Scanlon, his schoolboy team mate Paddy Kennedy, and a young lad called Duncan Edwards who had just made his Manchester United first team debut for the club against Cardiff City at Old Trafford. Duncan had actually become the third player in the final line up to have appeared in the senior Manchester United side, as Eddie Lewis and David Pegg had also done so.

A crowd of just under 21,000 was attracted to Old Trafford for an early evening game, no floodlights yet, on the first Monday of May 1953 to see if Matt Busby's young side could continue the exciting football they had produced throughout this first ever tournament, which included a still record 23-0 victory over Nantwich Town, and victories over Leeds United 4-0 (who included a certain Jack Charlton), Bury 2-0, Everton 1-0, Barnsley 3-1, Brentford 2-1 (a) and 6-0(h) over a two legged semi-final to reach the final against Stan Cullis's talented Wolverhampton Wanderers side.

Having won the League Championship in 1952 many felt that Manchester United side, having also won the FA Cup in 1948, was quickly coming to the end of their time, many of course, having lost seven years of their career due to the Second World War. Manager Matt Busby had quickly realised this of course, indeed, after the reserves had won the Central League in the first season after the war in the 1946/7 season, he had asked assistant manager Jimmy Murphy how many of that side would be able to step up. When the answer quickly came back as none, the pair of them set about creating a youth organisation which would not leave the club short in the future. The success of their work will be seen throughout this book...

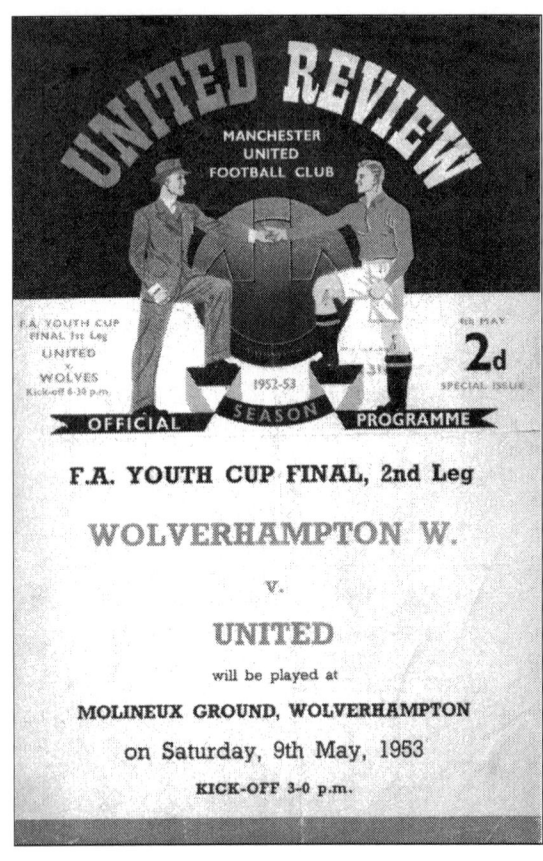

Wolverhampton Wanderers, under their brilliant manager Stan Cullis, had also identified young players as their future, with not picking up the local lad Duncan Edwards being a massive jolt to their overall progress. Edwards, from nearby Dudley, had actually nearly joined another Wanderers, Bolton, as his cousin Dennis Stevens was a player there along with Edwards England schoolboy International colleague Ray Parry. Matt Busby and Jimmy Murphy had gone out of their way to secure his signature and this new youth competition had showed the Edwards dominance as he took it by the scruff of the neck and hauled the side to the final. Wolves had actually not conceded a goal on their march to the final, but after only five minutes went a goal behind. A brilliant run by David Pegg, playing at inside left, left outside right McFarlane with an easy task to score. Within a minute though Wolves were on level terms when their centre forward Smith scored past United goalkeeper Gordon Clayton, who like Edwards was from the West Midlands, in Gordon's case Wednesbury.

Edwards, already at 5ft 10in and 12st a sixteen year old giant, quickly put his stamp all over the proceedings, storming throughout the field of play dominating the action. He linked brilliantly with the totally different in size to him Eddie Colman, but of the same boundless energy. By the twenty minute mark, Manchester United were 3-1 up thanks to goals from Eddie Lewis and David Pegg, which was the score at half time. McFarlane quickly added his second goal of the match before Lewis quickly did likewise to make it 5-1 before Albert Scanlon scored direct from a corner. All the night needed was a goal from the young Irish debutant, and with just six minutes to go, Billy Whelan provided it with a brilliant individual effort to leave the match, and tie, totally in Manchester United's favour at 7-1.

9th May
WOLVERHAMPTON WANDERERS v MANCHESTER UNITED
2nd Leg FA Youth Cup Final

The following Saturday, the sides took the field again, this time at Molyneux home of Wolverhampton Wanderers with the majority of the crowd of 15,000 hoping for a miracle, hopes which were raised when centre forward Smith repeated his first leg feat by scoring a very early goal for Wolves. The were up against, however, a really talented Manchester United side and their centre forward Eddie Lewis also repeated his first leg scoring knack by equalising on the day after half an hour or so, before the new Irish darling at inside right Billy Whelan, scored another goal after thirty seven minutes to confirm the name on the new trophy as being Manchester United. Smith did score again on the hour mark to draw the actual match at 2-2 but a 9-3 aggregate victory sent a firm message out to the football world that Manchester United had created a delivery line of success for the future. Their centre half Ronnie Cope went forward to lift the new FA Youth Cup, a trophy incidentally which would remain at Old Trafford for the first five years of the competition. The eleven players who represented the club in both ties were; Clayton, Fulton, Kennedy, Colman, Cope, Edwards, Mcfarlane, Whelan, Lewis, Pegg and Scanlon.

Billy Whelan actually was quickly back in his Irish roots with his new team mates as Manchester United took part in a ten day tour of Ireland, playing a game in Belfast and then matches in Dublin and Bray. They stayed first at the Hotel Pickie in Bangor

Northern Ireland before playing a friendly against the Boyland Youth Club, who had been strengthened by other local Belfast youngster's. A 3-0 victory was comfortably achieved before the squad travelled over the border staying at the International Hotel in Bray. There they were well received and looked after, particularly the three Irish lads in the squad, Paddy Kennedy, Noel McFarlane and of course, Billy Whelan. The first of the tour matches played in the Republic was at Tolka Park against a combination team made up of many local teams from the Dublin area. One of the players in the opposition was Vinnie Ryan, the player who originally Manchester United had been interested in. Another victory followed, this time by 4-1, with Billy heavily involved in a couple of the goals. The successful tour of Ireland was completed at the home of Bray Wanderers, where another combined team felt the full force of Manchester United, who ended off the visit with a crushing 6-0 victory.

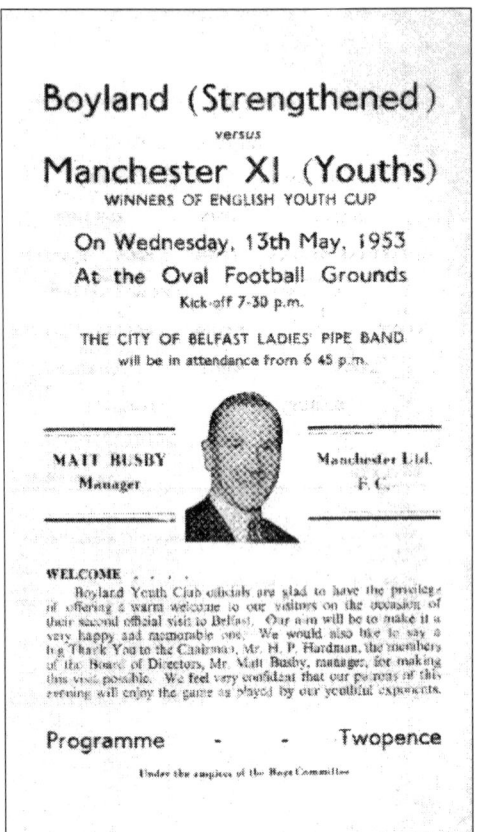

Whilst a bit disappointed in not scoring on his quick return to his homeland, with the season ended, Billy was able to gain his thoughts and prepare for his future away from his close family. His father, John, had died when Billy was only seven in 1942 leaving his mother Elizabeth to run a family home which consisted of older brother Christy, who took on the mantle of the man of the house, younger brother John and three sisters, Rita, Maura and Alice. That home was in St.Attracta Road Cabra, a suburb of Dublin, school was St Peter's in the shadow of Dalymount Park, the stadium which hosted all the top football matches in the country. The family's strong catholic faith held them together and brought them through, a faith which would be needed badly only five years on...

As a lad, Billy was a very talented Gaelic footballer also into Hurling in a big way winning medals at both, indeed, on one occasion being chosen to represent Dublin in both sports for competitions on the same day! He actually chose Gaelic football, but his Association Football was quickly brought to use at a junior side called the Red Rockets, and then at the age of thirteen at the local Home Farm Football Club, who had already produced Johnny Carey who had gone onto play and captain Manchester United and of course his country. Indeed, in 1946 when Billy Whelan was only eleven, Johnny Carey was captaining the Rest of Europe against Great Britain in a challenge match at Hampden Park, two years later making all Ireland even prouder as he lifted the FA Cup for Manchester United in the memorable 1948 final against Blackpool. By 1952, as Carey then lifted the League Championship for Manchester United, again all the folk back home in Ireland were ever so proud, although a seventeen year old Billy Whelan must have wondered if his tilt at football stardom was escaping him, especially as it has been pointed out that a few of his team mates in the Eire Boys team had crossed the Irish Sea to play for English clubs.

Billy had incredible individual skills, his smooth running, allied to brilliant footwork, marvellous thought of mind and deadly goal scoring ability put him as an outstanding all round footballer from an early age. He must have had doubts though, he had played in lots of trophy winning side whilst with Eire Boys, and the caps followed for the Eire Youth International side. A year later, the unfortunate injury to John Doherty finally opened a door for young Billy, and he was in no mood to let it close, he was determined to show Matt Busby and Jimmy Murphy that he fully deserved his opportunity.

Chapter Two
So This is Manchester

Having spent the summer with his family, home in Dublin, it was time for Billy to get his bearings in his 'new' home of Manchester. Like many of the younger players brought to Manchester by Matt Busby and Jimmy Murphy in search of their rebuilding of Manchester United after the Second World War, and despite winning both League and Cup, realising that the supply chain to follow was not there, Billy was put in lodgings. His were with Mrs Watson based near the 'other' Old Trafford, the cricket ground home of Lancashire County Cricket Club, also close to the big open spaces of Longford Park. All this was, in reality, a short walk up the road, crossing Chester Road and down Warwick Road to the football stadium. Mrs Watson, like others, was chosen by Matt and Jimmy to bring that home from home feeling that young lads coming from various regions of Britain would need to help them settle and produce the football skills that had been spotted close to their maternal homes. One of the first lads Billy would meet was a young lad called Bobby Charlton who had just come from Ashington in the North East, whose brother Jack was already into a football career over the Pennines at Leeds. Other players already at Mrs Watson's were David Pegg and Tommy Taylor, two Yorkshire lads, David from Doncaster and Tommy, who had actually been a record signing for Manchester United at the time, who came from Barnsley. Billy would actually have three landladies in his time in Manchester, as he would move onto lodge with Mrs Gibbs and finally the Dolan family, who were friends of his brother Christy, and lived over in the Stockport area. It was there that he felt nearer home than anywhere else in Manchester.

Like elsewhere in Britain, Manchester was still recovering from the Second World War in the early 1950's. In 1953 Billy Whelan would be around in a pivotal year which saw the Coronation of Princess Elizabeth to Queen Elizabeth11, Mount Everest was conquered, Roger Bannister running the first sub four minute mile, England regaining the Ashes from Australia, and as mentioned earlier, the famous Stanley Matthews FA Cup Final victory for Blackpool over Bolton Wanderers. There were still major logistic problems around however, rationing was still in place (until 1954) whilst despite plentiful employment, because of the severe bombing of major cities such as Manchester, re building was desperately needed. Close by to Old Trafford was the sprawling Trafford Park complex of factories, with trains moving materials around and smoke filling the whole atmosphere. A little further along, over the Trafford Road Bridge, was the Salford Docks which continued to operate until the 1960's. Remember also that in those days there was very little Television, never mind no twitter, Facebook, mobile phones etc, to gather information from. Radio's and Newspapers were the two main themes, with in Manchester, two Evening Papers the Evening News and the Evening Chronicle.

Those two papers and the excellent 'United Review' club programme of Manchester United would be where the name of Billy Whelan would be seen, although references back to Liam Whelan was also made. The 1953/4 season would see Billy involved in the junior sides who played matches in the Lancashire League, the Manchester League and the Altrincham Junior League. He also featured in a prestigious challenge match as the FA Youth Cup winners in Manchester United played the FA County Youth Cup winners, who were Sheffield & Hallamshire. Sheffield though, had a very decent side which included players such as Alan Hodgkinson the Sheffield United goalkeeper who would eventually play for England, and Tony Kay the Sheffield Wednesday half back who later was a real star at Everton and played for England, before his career was destroyed due to his implication in the betting scandal which engulfed football in the early 1960's. The match in September 1953 was played at Old Trafford with United winning another trophy, this time 7-0. The benefits of full time training enabled Billy to grow stronger and by October of 1953 those benefits were becoming evident. From that month until January 1954, Billy scored twenty nine goals from nineteen matches, which, although he was now too old to play in the FA Youth Cup, promotion to the Central League reserve team would be the next step up. All the time he would be under the watchful eye of Jimmy Murphy seeing how he would react to the physical side of the games, with in the reserves certainly coming up against hardened old pros who may be coming back from injury or seeing out careers. It was not for the faint hearted, although all the backroom staff immediately saw the silky skills from the young Irishman whose added gift of scoring regular goals was also a massive asset.

Off the field he was, obviously, still getting used to the difference from the Dublin suburbs to life right in a major city, and also being right in the limelight as a player for Manchester United. Both Jimmy Murphy and Matt Busby were, however, always keen to see just how far their younger players could be tested at higher levels and in early December 1953, Billy was given that opportunity when a Manchester United XI was to play the Western Command in a friendly over in Wales at the home of Wrexham's Racecourse stadium. With men having to serve their National Service from eighteen for a couple of years, teams such as Western Command would include footballers doing their National Service alongside other young, fit personnel. For this game such as Mel Hopkins full back of Tottenham Hotspur and later Wales, Jimmy Meadows a fine Manchester City full back, Norman Deeley a small dynamic winger, part of the upcoming Wolverhampton Wanderers side and right half Ronnie Clayton, not only a future Blackburn Rovers captain but also a future regular England International. Matt Busby reacted to this type of opposition by playing nine players who had first team experience, alongside two younger lads, left back Geoff Bent and Bill Whelan playing in his favoured inside right number eight shirt. Four of those older players who had played first team football included, Jack Crompton in goal, John Aston at full back, Henry Cockburn at left half and the quite brilliant Stan Pearson at inside left, all who had won both the FA Cup and the League Championship inside the past five seasons. In the end, two goals from Pearson and two from centre forward Eddie Lewis, who had played alongside Billy in the recent FA Youth Cup Final, sealed a 4-1 victory for United.

Continuing his progress, Billy's debut in the reserves came at the end of January 1954 with his natural skills and goal scoring continuing to blossom, soon a hat trick away at Derby County being the proof he was able to compete. It would be the end of the season before Billy Whelan was suddenly elevated back into the news as he was included in another strong looking Manchester United side for a friendly at Norwich City and then to be the star of the clubs first victory in the prestigious Blue Star youth tournament in Switzerland. The Norwich City fixture was for the Jubilee of the Norfolk and Norwich Charities Cup played at their Carrow Road ground, twelve months after Billy Whelan had played his first Manchester United match in the FA Youth Cup Final. It was certainly the strongest United side he had appeared in, with his fellow forwards being England International's Johnny Berry, Tommy Taylor and Jack Rowley, with another fantastic footballer, Dennis Viollet, making up the forward five. Sadly for Billy and United, Second Division Norwich responded to meeting their famous opponents and won the match, and local cup, 2-1 with Viollet getting a late consolation goal for United.

Within days, Billy was to get the opportunity of playing with younger stars of Manchester United, and Europe, as the club took part in their first ever Blue Star youth tournament in Switzerland. It was a side made up of the side that had successfully defended the FA Youth Cup, beating Wolverhampton Wanderers for the second successive season, with Duncan Edwards, Eddie Colman, David Pegg and Albert Scanlon, having been joined by even younger players Wilf McGuinness and Bobby Charlton and slightly older ones such as Billy and Ian Greaves. The competition comprised of matches played of thirty minutes in total, fifteen each way. After an opening 0-0 draw with a local side, United quickly accustomed themselves to the surroundings in Switzerland, beating Berne Boys 2-0 and Blue Star Zurich 1-0, before a single goal from Billy was enough to beat MTV Munich and earn a final place. This would be against the local Blue Star side who they had already beat to this final spot, only this time they won with ease 4-0 with Duncan Edwards scoring a hat trick.

Having won this prestigious trophy, Manchester United played a couple of important friendlies before they returned home. The first was a personal highlight for Billy as he scored five goals as United beat a Berne select side 9-2 and then he stared in an emphatic 4-0 victory over the Swiss National Youth side, scoring yet another goal, a match which was played before a crowd of 42,000 who had assembled for the Switzerland v Holland full International match which followed. 1954 saw also the World Cup being staged in Switzerland and such was Billy Whelan's skills in being instrumental in Manchester United winning the trophy, then beating the host National Youth side 4-0, he was incredibly the centre of attention from officials from Santos the famous Brazilian side over in Switzerland for the forthcoming World Cup, who enquired about the possibility of signing Billy from United, such was his outstanding talent in the competition. When you think another four years on, Santos would provide a certain Pele to help win Brazil their first World Cup, who knows where Billy Whelan's life would have turned out?

The magnitude of Manchester United winning this tournament, which had been dubbed the 'Mini World Cup', ensured the whole party being treated to a reception at Manchester Town Hall by the Lord Mayor on their return home.

Chapter Three
First Team Debut

Back to reality after the glamour of winning the 'mini World Cup' and being chased by one of Brazil's greatest ever sides, Billy regrouped home in Dublin before returning for what promised to be a pivotal season for him at Manchester United. That it started in their 'A' team and finished with him playing seven matches in the first team towards the end of the season showed how far that progress had gone.

Four goals in two 'A' team fixtures earned Billy promotion to the Central League team, with him scoring six goals in his first seven appearances, including two against Liverpool Reserves, their first team being in the Second Division in those days. Big victories over Leeds United 6-2 with two goals from Billy and 5-0 against Blackburn Rovers in early January 1955 when Billy's goal was then his eleventh in nineteen appearances showed the consistent finishing he was displaying.

In this 1954/55 season, the changing of the guard was very evident at Old Trafford as Matt Busby and Jimmy Murphy continued to see older, established stars of the post war era leave or retire, whilst their younger breed was being nurtured in the juniors and reserve side, along of course with their success in the FA Youth Cup, continuing to be seen. True greats of Manchester United such as Johnny Carey, Allenby Chilton, Henry Cockburn, Stan Pearson and Jack Rowley would all have left by the end of the season. The more regular XI now included; Wood, Foulkes, Byrne, Gibson, Jones, Edwards, Berry, Taylor, Viollet and either Pegg or Scanlon. The one shirt which was up for grabs was the number eight, inside right position which was, of course, the one Billy Whelan wanted to occupy. Jackie Blanchflower had been given many outings, although in fairness to Jackie, he was such a great footballer that he could play in the number four, five, six and ten shirts as well, so often got moved about.

By March 1955 Billy Whelan was about to be given his real opportunity for that number eight shirt, although in the month he would actually go from playing games in the 'A' team, the reserve side, in a couple of first team friendlies and then finally his debut in a First Division match for Manchester United. The month of March 1955 went as follows for Billy Whelan;

Saturday 5th. A match for the 'A' team at Irlam against Lancashire Steel, one of the biggest employers in the area. The 'A' team were on a great run scoring goals for fun, indeed, in the eight matches they had played since January 1st they had won them all and scored sixty six goals in the process! Another nine was added in the match at Irlam, with Billy getting his customary goal.

Saturday 12th. Whilst Billy had played in Manchester United sides which had included a lot of first team players such as his games against Western Command and Norwich City the previous season, a week after playing at Irlam against Lancashire Steel for

the 'A' team, he was included in a full first team who played a friendly at then Second Division Lincoln City at their Sincil Bank ground. He was the only alteration to the United side that had beat Burnley 1-0 in the First Division and he was actually replacing the goal scorer that day, Duncan Edwards, who was included in the FA Youth Cup side playing at Old Trafford against Plymouth Argyle. It can be seen just how much Matt Busby and Jimmy Murphy wanted to continue their retention of that trophy by this decision, but Billy Whelan was certainly not arguing, this was his real chance to shine at the highest level. It was, therefore, a real shock to everybody's system when Lincoln City went two goals in front late in the first half, before Colin Webster struck twice in two minutes to equalise by half time. A winning goal from Albert Scanlon at least gave Billy the satisfaction of coming away with a victory despite him playing in the more unfamiliar number ten position.

Saturday 19th. With Duncan Edwards return from youth team duty, it was back to the Central League for Billy and an away fixture at Stoke City. The reserves were only two points off the top spot, but a surprise 3-2 defeat did not help their chances of a title.

Wednesday 22nd. Another match against the Western Command saw a much more reserve type line up played by Manchester United for the match at the home of Ashton Untied. Billy Whelan though really relished the chance to impress Matt Busby and Jimmy Murphy and stole the show with a brilliant hat trick as United won 6-0 which was to win him his coveted actual first team debut in the Football League the following Saturday.

Saturday 26th. Deepdale, home of Preston North End the previous seasons FA Cup losing finalists, was to be the venue for Billy's full debut for Manchester United on a pitch inches deep in mud. A surprisingly small crowd of just over 13,000 were present to witness it, although as Preston's favourite son, Tom Finney was unfit the locals probably decided to save their hard earned money. A future name for Manchester United followers, Tommy Docherty, was in a still strong Preston side but Billy was able to prove to everyone just how good a player he was as United eased to a 2-0 victory thanks to goals from Scanlon and Byrne. The Manchester United side for Billy Whelan's full debut was; Wood, Foulkes, Byrne, Gibson, Jones, Whitefoot, Berry, Whelan, Taylor, Edwards and Scanlon.

As Billy had won the shirt on merit, the next task was to keep it, and he was given a bit of a run in the side playing the next six fixtures against Sheffield United, Sunderland home and away over the Easter break, Leicester City, West Bromwich Albion, and the eventual FA Cup winners of 1955, Newcastle

United. The first of those was at the beginning of April against Sheffield United at Old Trafford, on the same day as Duncan Edwards made his full England debut against Scotland in a 2-1 victory at Wembley Stadium. Billy also had something to celebrate as he scored his first Manchester United senior goal, on the day after his twentieth birthday, as they turned on all the style in the second half to overwhelm Sheffield United 5-0. This was to also be the first time that the Manchester United inside forward trio would be Whelan, Taylor and Viollet. Soon they would be the most feared trio of forwards in all of England. Billy was quoted of that feeling of scoring his first Manchester United goal by saying. "What a feeling I had, something I could never hope to describe. It seemed I was going to burst with pride".

After the Newcastle United match, Matt Busby decided to take Billy out of the firing line with him missing the last three fixtures, Manchester United finishing the season in eighth place, but everybody could see the evolution of Manchester United from the 1948 and 1952 trophy winners into an exciting young side. This could also be seen throughout the club, as the reserves finished runners up, Billy actually getting sixteen goals in twenty six matches, whilst all three junior sides won their leagues and the FA Youth Cup was won for the third consecutive season. Whilst Billy might have only scored one goal in his seven first team appearances, his all round play, linking the midfield and making openings for others, along with his obvious goal scoring threat, marked him down as a real find.

The last league match of the season incidentally was against the actual league winners that season, Chelsea. I went to the game with my late father Albert, taking a spot on the Stretford End as United won 2-1 to record a double over the new champions. After the game my father took me round to the old player's entrance halfway down what is now the Munich Tunnel. As the Chelsea players came out he said hang on here, took my autograph book and promptly got onto their coach, which also promptly drove away with my dad on it! As I forlornly made my way towards the concourse, I saw the coach stop, with my dad getting off walking back to meet me with all the new champions autographs in my prized book!

Although the league season had ended, the week after Newcastle United beat Manchester City 3-1 in the Wembley FA Cup Final, as a full strength Manchester United party was touring Denmark and Sweden. Billy Whelan was included by Matt Busby in the squad which won all four matches played, with Billy getting into the team for the last match against a very strong Gothenburg team. He scored a goal late in the second half of the match, which United won 4-2, but before he was able to travel home to Dublin to enjoy his summer with his family, Billy was again involved in the Blue Star youth tournament in Switzerland. The year before it had been tagged the 'Mini World Cup' and United again reached the final, only this time losing by 1-0 to Italian side Genoa. They went onto Wolfsburg in Germany to play in a prestigious tournament there winning the final 7-0 against a French side. Such was United's display that the President of the French team said that the display was the best he had ever seen by a youth side. Of the eleven matches United played in Switzerland and Germany they won ten only losing that final to Genoa. They also scored sixty three goals conceding only five. The team that won the trophy in Germany was; Clayton, Lewis, Beswick, Colman, Jones (P), McGuinness, Scanlon, Whelan, Doherty, Charlton and Pegg. Bobby Charlton with an hat trick and two goals apiece from Billy and Albert Scanlon won the final in Germany, and as you can see from the forward line alone this was a very exciting Manchester United eleven.

As a footnote to United's role in the Blue Star competition in Switzerland, which still continues nowadays, they have actually won it eighteen times in total, far and away more than any other side, Barcelona winning it three times for example. The competition has provided invaluable experience for young players to travel to Europe and see the different standard of play, with after the Busby Babes, the likes of George Best, Norman Whiteside, Mark Hughes and The Class of 92 all playing in it for Manchester United.

Chapter Four
Double Championships for Billy

Billy Whelan had an incredible season in 1955/56, playing enough matches to actually win League Championships in TWO leagues, the First Division and the Central League. He would play twenty five matches in the reserves, scoring twenty goals, whilst in the first team in league appearances he played thirteen matches scoring four goals The position he was aiming for, inside right number eight, was probably the most contested of the eleven. In Billy's case he had John Doherty, Jackie Blanchflower and Colin Webster and sometimes even Dennis Viollet who would be switched to put Duncan Edwards at inside left. Billy, therefore, had a lot of challenges and knew when that chance came again he just had to take it.

Scoring goals was a big priority, and Billy started the season in the reserves really well. He scored three goals in the first five matches before he was hastily called into the first team at Sheffield United's Bramall Lane ground after Duncan Edwards succumbed to the flu bug sweeping Britain. An unlucky own goal from centre half Mark Jones settled the match but Billy stayed in the side for the midweek game at Goodison Park against Everton, as even more call offs affected the first team. Duncan Edwards was still missing, indeed, his bout of flu seemed to be far worse than that, as he spent a few days in Park Hospital Urmston. A very young forward line which included Billy, Doherty, Lewis and Pegg relinquished a 2-1 half time lead at Everton to eventually lose 4-2.

Sadly, as those results went against United, Billy was moved back into the reserves as the established players returned, but Billy quickly got amongst the goals again with the winner in the reserve match at Everton and two goals in a 7-1 thrashing of Barnsley at Old Trafford where a large crowd saw the reserves go clear at the top of their table. That position was emphasised when the side went over the Pennines to play Leeds United at Elland Road with Billy having a superb match, scoring a hat trick and also laying on a goal for young Bobby Charlton in a 4-0 victory. This was Billy's ninth goal in eight reserve matches, incidentally, it was also Bobby Charlton's ninth goal in his nine appearances, and Bobby was then playing as an out and out centre forward, number nine.

The first team also started to go on a winning run playing excellent, attacking football with as November arrived they joined the reserves as being top of their league. Manchester United supporters responded to the fine football being played, the reserves for example attracting a crowd of over 7,000 for the visit of Blackpool to witness a 4-0 victory, Billy with two of the goals. This display prompted one scout from a decent side to reflect that he would play them in their entirety in his own club's league side!

I went to my first ever away match of Manchester United in this month of November 1955 when my late father Albert took me to Bolton Wanderers, sadly, to see them lose their first match since the Everton game as Bolton won 3-1, although it was great to see the debut of my fellow Salfordian Eddie Colman. Eddie had been a team mate of Billy Whelan since his first ever Manchester United game back in 1953 at the FA Youth Cup Final and his inclusion on merit must have continued to increase Billy's desire to also become that on merit.

On the day we were at Bolton, the reserves beat Chesterfield 5-0 at Old Trafford with Bobby Charlton getting two of the goals against a young Chesterfield goalkeeper called Gordon Banks. Just over ten years later the two of them would be in the same England side when they beat West Germany in the 1966 World Cup Final at Wembley.

As Christmas approached, Billy scored his thirteenth goal in only seventeen reserve matches when they beat Wolverhampton Wanderers 4-0 at Old Trafford. Christmas Day matches were still in the calendar, although with that being a Sunday in 1955, and football most definitely not on the agenda in those days, United had matches on Christmas Eve, Boxing Day and the day after, three games in four days! Two of the games for the reserves were home and away against local side Bury, with the results being 6-1(a) and 7-1(h) victories. Billy got a total of three of those goals, scoring again away at Maine Road against Manchester City in a 3-0 victory taking his total to seventeen in twenty two matches, just needing that break back into the first team. Interestingly, on the day Billy played at Maine Road for the reserves, his profile picture appeared on the cover of the United Review match programme for the first team match at Old Trafford.

That first team call up was not far away, although he actually got it from a surprise 4-0 defeat for the first team away at then Second Division Bristol Rovers in the FA Cup 3rd round tie. The shock waves went around football and John Doherty was one of the casualties, John again giving another avenue to success at Manchester United for Billy Whelan. John, of course, had suffered injury on the eve of the first ever FA Youth Cup Final against Wolverhampton Wanderers to hasten Billy Whelan's arrival in Manchester, the dropping this time of John Doherty was the break Billy needed. He took it...

Sheffield United continued to play an important part of Billy's career. A year earlier he had scored his first ever senior Manchester United goal in a 5-0 victory at Old Trafford, earlier this 1955/56 season he had been thrown in as a late replacement for Duncan Edwards for the Bramall Lane fixture and here he was, in mid January 1956, beginning his real attempt at being the first choice Manchester United number

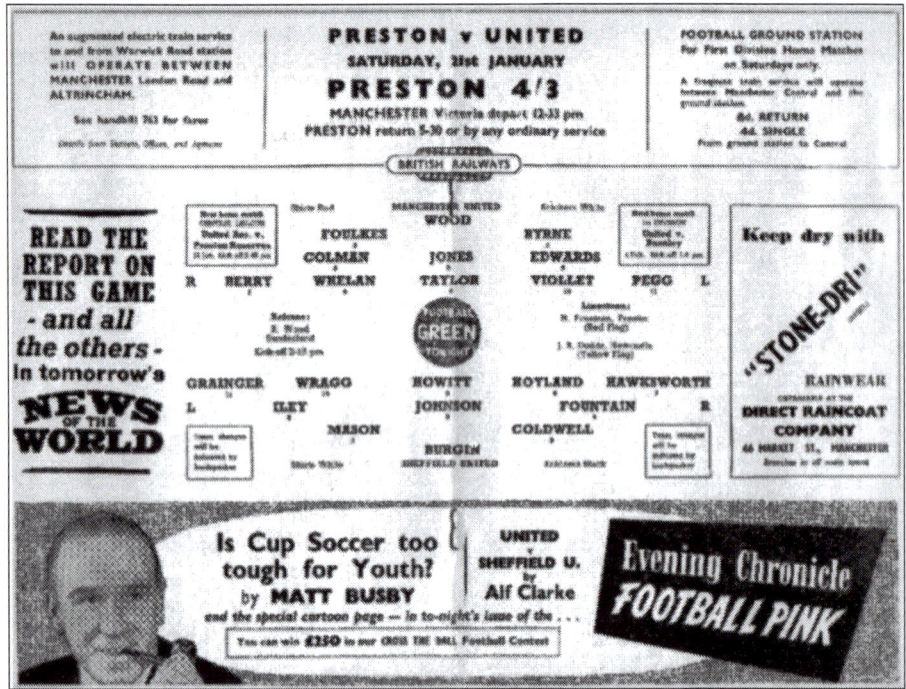

eight. A crowd of just over 30,000 saw United win 3-1, interestingly, this was the first time that the eleven I always associated as the first eleven of Matt Busby's 'Busby Babes' took a field as a unit. They were; Wood, Foulkes, Byrne, Colman, Jones, Edwards, Berry, Whelan, Taylor, Viollet and Pegg. The week after came another pivotal moment for Billy, he was in the side that lost 3-1 at Preston North End, but Billy got the only United goal and despite that defeat Matt Busby knew this was the side that was ready for senior honours. He was right. An undefeated run until the end of the season, fourteen league fixtures in total, saw Manchester United to their second post war League Championship.

Because they had been knocked out of the FA Cup in the 3rd round, Manchester United had a spare Saturday at the end of January, so travelled over to Leeds to play a friendly against a side who were then in the Second Division. Billy had a couple of efforts cleared off the line but United eased to a 4-1 victory with John Charles having an outstanding match for the home side. Having in later life wrote the biography of Duncan Edwards, I am often asked was there anybody who compared to him, well in my opinion, the only one I saw to come close was John Charles who played with ease as either centre half or centre forward and, of course, was also a fine Wales International under their managership of Manchester United assistant manager Jimmy Murphy.

Despite that defeat at Preston North End, Manchester United were still at the top of the table, and when they went onto a five match winning run, not conceding in four of them, they showed they certainly meant to stay there. Burnley at home and Luton Town and Wolverhampton Wanderers away were all beaten 2-0, with Billy scoring in the match at Luton and also having a fine match in the vital win at Wolverhampton.

When Aston Villa arrived at Old Trafford at the end of February, United were six points clear of second placed Blackpool, and in a very strong position. A single goal victory, and that it was scored by Billy, showed the impact he was making on the side now, feeling really comfortable with his surroundings in the team and contributing to a high level. That fine Manchester United historian, Tom Clare who now lives in America, wrote a fine piece on Billy Whelan for MUST, the independent Manchester United supporter's organisation, relating a tale about Billy given to Tom by a friend who had attended the Aston Villa match. Evidentially the person was then only just ten and still remembered the fact that it chucked it down with rain, remember Old Trafford was mainly an open stadium in those days, and recalls Billy scoring the only goal. What made even more impression on him was that, as most boys of the time, getting autographs was nearly as important as seeing the game! He stood outside the old player's entrance, halfway down where the Munich Tunnel is now, and as the players made a dash because of the heavy rain, he still recalls Billy Whelan taking the time to sign all those there wanting those vital autographs. Billy, in his belted grey gabardine mac and a trilby hat jauntily dripping rain all over the books. That United had won 1-0 was important, that that young lad also got the goal scorers autograph and he had taken the time to talk to him was a moment to live through a person's life. Incidentally, when that truly great footballer Johan Cruyff sadly passed away in March 2016, Tom also recalled that Billy Whelan, and other greats like Tom Finney, had produced the turn that became known as the 'Cruyff turn' in the 1950's, but due to the lack of television coverage it was not seen.

A brilliant victory 4-2 at the home of the previous season's champions Chelsea, showed all the country, particularly the critical London press, that this new, young vibrant Manchester United, were on the verge of being this season's champions. Two 1-1 draws followed, surprisingly at home to Cardiff City, then away at Highbury home of Arsenal. Whilst United were in London for that match, I was at Old Trafford in a crowd of over 23,000 to see the latest FA Youth team play Bexley & Welling, who were the junior side of Charlton Athletic, and witnessed a 11-1 victory with Bobby Charlton scoring five of those goals in a brilliant personal display alongside yet another fine youth team performance from Manchester United. As all this was going on, news from Arsenal was coming via the old scoreboard behind the open end, although that could not tell us of a missed Roger Byrne penalty which would have brought all the points home. Still, five points clear with only seven matches left kept United in a brilliant position.

Billy suffered an injury in the home match with Bolton Wanderers, enforcing Matt Busby to make his first team change in ten weeks when Newcastle United arrived at Old Trafford, with John Doherty stepping back into the side seamlessly, scoring a brilliant goal as United won easily 5-2. This injury cost Billy vital matches, including the incredible League Championship decider when they beat their only challenger, Blackpool 2-1 at Old Trafford. Although I was only nine, I was going to more matches at Old Trafford, this vital game I was asked by one of my uncle's did I want to go with him. Did I want to go? You bet! So off we went over the Trafford Road swing bridge from near where I lived off Ordsall Lane, buying a programme outside the ground, only to see people desperately trying to get in at the scoreboard end. We went around to the Stretford End, finally just getting in with thousands locked out. Climbing up the steps to the top, I was suddenly faced with everybody's back sides, so as a little nine year old having no chance of seeing the match. I can still remember turning round and seeing the works side Glovers Cables playing a match on their works pitch behind the still open ended Stretford End!

Forty eight hours after winning the League Championship, Manchester United were off to Scotland to play a friendly at Dundee, with Billy Whelan fit enough to join the party. Actually party is the appropriate word as the team had enjoyed themselves into the early hours after the Blackpool victory and some struggled to even catch the 9.30am train up to Scotland. With the added fact that Roger Byrne, Duncan Edwards and Tommy Taylor had gone elsewhere in Scotland to prepare for the forthcoming Scotland v England International, it meant a rather fragile Manchester United side. Things did not get better when the match started at Dens Park Dundee when goalkeeper Ray Wood was injured and had to go off, with it being a friendly a substitute was allowed and it was Billy who came on. His Irish friend and team mate Paddy Kennedy, making a rare appearance in the first eleven, took over in goal but the end result of 5-1 to Dundee was probably to be expected in all the circumstances.

Billy got back into the first team for the away match at Sunderland, scoring one of United's goals in a 2-2 draw with the title won and only one more match left in the season. There was, however, one really important match left for Billy Whelan as Manchester United travelled over the Irish Sea to play a friendly in Billy's home city of Dublin and against his former club Home Farm.

Home Farm Football Club had been founded in 1928, with the likes of Johnny Carey and Billy Whelan being brilliant success for the club as we reached the end of the

1955/56 season, now providing two players to win League Championships for Manchester United. Another local Irish lad, left back Joe Carolan had just joined United at this time, soon to be joined by Johnny Giles. Manchester United took a fairly strong side over to Home Farm, with only Roger Byrne, Duncan Edwards and Eddie Colman missing from the title winning team. Home Farm though had Irish International players from Everton and Fulham to supplement their side, along with Bolton Wanderers centre forward Nat Lofthouse for the match at Dalymount Park. This was a great opportunity for Billy Whelan to show the folk back home how far he had progressed, particularly with a national side to be selected for the friendly with Holland coming up. Billy did not disappoint, scoring the opening goal in United's 4-1 victory and generally being man of the match. An after match dinner at the Red Bank Restaurant in Dublin must have tasted very sweet to local boy Billy.

Billy's display did, indeed, impress and he received his first call up for the Republic of Ireland side for the match against Holland which was to be played at Feyenoord's Rotterdam Stadium. The International team were managed by Johnny Carey, so the link with Manchester United for Billy was there to see, with future United personnel of different forms, Noel Cantwell as a future captain and Frank O'Farrell as a future manager also in the side. Before all this though, Manchester United were presented with the League title at the last match of the season against Portsmouth at Old Trafford, with Billy proudly receiving his second title medal, having also received his Central League one. United were then off to Scandinavia for another post season tour.

Appearances, and goals, in Gothenburg and Copenhagen for Manchester United, gave Billy further work out's before he left the United tour and travelled across to Holland. A crowd of 60,000 saw a tight goalless first half before Ireland turned on some real skills in the second, with Billy playing the schemer's role to perfection as

Fitsimmons with two, Haverty and Ringstead won the match 4-1. A fine start to what seemed to be the beginning of a long, distinguished International career beckoning for Billy Whelan.

He was also now Manchester United's regular number eight, part of a brilliant young side who would be seeing more of Europe themselves the following season as the club entered the European Cup as England's first ever representatives.

Chapter Five
The World is your Oyster

Season 1956/57 promised to be the biggest in the history of Manchester United. Their increased pool of players, having been supplemented by a fantastic youth system, was going to be tested to the full with the defence of their newly won League Championship, a real tilt at the FA Cup which had not been at Old Trafford since 1948, and their involvement in the European Cup which was only its second year itself. The previous season the champions of Spain, Real Madrid had won the first European Cup, when England's representation, Chelsea, had acceded to the view of the Football League that they did not enter. That same organisation also 'told' Manchester United not to enter, Matt Busby, however, was not for turning, he knew that he had an exceptional group of players and testing them even further with European experience was the next stage in their development.

The accepted first team at Manchester United at the start of the season was; Wood, Foulkes, Byrne, Colman, Jones, Edwards, Berry, Whelan, Taylor, Viollet and Pegg. Matt Busby though, knew he had an excellent replacement for each position. Perhaps goalkeeper was the only position of concern although Jack Crompton was still on the books and Gordon Clayton promised to be a fine keeper. At full back, Ian Greaves and Geoff Bent would be first choice anywhere else, the half back reserves included Freddie Goodwin, also a Lancashire County Cricketer, Ronnie Cope or Jackie Blanchflower at centre half, and Wilf McGuinness at left half. Jackie Blanchflower, of course, not just a centre half possibility he could play with ease at right half, left half and both inside right and left as well. For replacement forwards Matt Busby had such as Colin Webster who could, and did, play all across the line, John Doherty who must have looked at Billy Whelan and thought why not me?, young forwards such as Bobby Charlton and Alex Dawson who scored for fun and in Albert Scanlon a left winger who would also be first choice anywhere else. A rich group indeed, with further down the next conveyor belt in full swing with names in the 'A', 'B' and Junior sides at the start of the 1956/57 season including such as Dave Gaskell, Shay Brennan, Joe Carolan, Mark Pearson, Kenny Morgans and Johnny Giles who would eventually all play for Manchester United first team.

That sort of squad would be needed as, in total, Manchester United would be faced with fifty seven first team matches, covering the League Championship, FA Cup, European Cup and a Charity Shield fixture. Billy Whelan would feature in fifty four of these fixtures and he would be the club's top scorer with thirty three goals. To show how prolific his goal scoring was, Billy scored in the first six away matches and at one stage had scored in eight consecutive league matches. He was truly now a vital part of the side known as 'The Busby Babes'

So, all was in place as Birmingham City visited Old Trafford for the first game of the season, although there was a serious chance of it being called off as torrential rain fell on the ground, and this, in theory, still part of a British summer! United went 1-0 up against the previous season's losing FA Cup finalists (Birmingham had lost 3-1 to Manchester City at Wembley) but it took a second half equaliser from Dennis Viollet to share the spoils. As I said, Billy had a fine goal scoring start to the season, scoring in six away matches on the trot at Preston North End, West Bromwich Albion (a last minute headed winner), Chelsea, Newcastle United, Arsenal and Sunderland. Five of those games were won with only a draw at Newcastle United spoiling a complete set of victories. Billy also, of course, had a liking for scoring at Old Trafford as well and with goals against Sheffield Wednesday, Manchester City, Charlton Athletic and Everton he was, at one stage also on an eight match consecutive league goal scoring spree, from the Chelsea away until the Everton at home games consecutively. With ten victories and only two draws in the first twelve league games Manchester United were also already clear at the top of the league as they defended their title win of the previous season.

I was at the Everton match which produced one of the most amazing matches of the Busby Babes era as table topping United lost at home 5-2 to a side five places off bottom of the table! Bobby Charlton scored the other United goal in this match, his second appearance in the first team, the first being the previous home match against his namesake side Charlton Athletic, which United had won 4-2 with Bobby scoring two alongside goals from Billy and Dennis Viollet. In the week running up to this match, Billy had made his second International appearance against Denmark, this time in his home city of Dublin with the locals seeing a 2-1 victory

Billy Whelan had become used to European experience in his three year career at Old Trafford, friendlies at the end of the season in Sweden and Denmark, along with youth matches in Germany and Switzerland had made him quite a traveller. When you add his International debut in Holland, the arrival of the European Cup did not leave him star struck. His first two travels were to Belgium and Germany for ties with Anderlecht and Dortmund Borussia respectively. Anderlecht were defeated 2-0 in their home leg before they arrived in Manchester to play the second leg, but not at Old Trafford, it was Maine Road home of local rivals Manchester City that the game took place under floodlights. The lack of those lights at Old Trafford necessitated this move across the city for a night that will, forever, remain in Manchester United's history. On a very wet night, United took a decent side in Anderlecht apart by the score line of 10-0. Billy got into the act with two goals mid way through the second half, although they were numbers seven and eight by then! Most of the forwards got in the act with Viollet getting four, Taylor three, Billy his two and Johnny Berry one, whilst the one forward who did not score, left winger David Pegg was the man who laid most of them on.

This crushing 12-0 aggregate victory, earned United a two legged tie with German Champions Dortmund and when United went 3-0 up in the first leg, again played at Maine Road, thoughts were on another avalanche of goals. The German side were a very experienced team however, and they slowly came back into the match finally bringing the score back to 3-2 in United's favour, and the prospect of a difficult second leg in Germany. That it was, but this time it was strong defending, with goalkeeper Ray Wood, full back's Billy Foulkes and Roger Byrne and centre half Mark Jones all having outstanding matches as United held out for a 0-0 draw and a quarter final place in the New Year.

In between the two Dortmund ties, Billy picked up another winners medal, that of the Charity Shield as United played under the Maine Road floodlights again, only this time against City as the previous season's Champions and Cup Winners played out a match which United won 1-0. There is an interesting story from David Gaskell, then a very junior United goalkeeper, about this match. Dave was in digs with Billy and Duncan Edwards at the time, and when he got back to those digs after his cleaning duties at Old Trafford, his two senior team mates had gone off to Maine Road for the game. Dave had his tea and decided to get a bus across town to see the match. Early on in the match, Ray Wood was injured and Duncan Edwards took over in goal, before somebody from the club spotted Dave sat in the stand, told him to get into some kit and take his place! There was no official substitutions in those days, but the two managers, Matt Busby and Les McDowell had agreed to use them for a goalkeeper. Dave had a mad dash looking for kit before taking his place between the sticks and helping United win 1-0. He took a lot of ribbing from Billy and Duncan after the match, although they were, naturally, delighted that Dave had helped United secure another trophy. Incidentally, Dave Gaskell is still the youngest Manchester United player to take part in a competitive match.

Billy's outstanding run of scoring league goals ended with the match at Blackpool, the side who had chased United for the league title the previous season, which ended 2-2 and kept United at the top of the table. He was back on the goal trail the week after though as United beat Wolverhampton Wanderers 3-0 at Old Trafford. What would be the expected defeat at Bolton Wanderers, this time 2-0, cost United the lead for the first time this season to Tottenham Hotspur and the two sides were due to meet in London on the Saturday after the second leg European Cup tie in Germany against Dortmund. Before that, Billy scored two goals as United beat a John Charles inspired Leeds United at Old Trafford.

When United met Tottenham at White Hart Lane in the top of the table match, Billy was involved in an unusual situation. Manchester United, obviously, wanted Billy in their team, especially as he had by then scored fourteen goals from his seventeen matches in the league, but the day after on the Sunday the Republic of Ireland were playing World Cup holders Germany in a prestigious friendly in Dublin and desperately wanted their new, young star inside forward in the side. With it being a friendly, Billy was kept in London and duly played his part in a magnificent match which ended 2-2 with United coming back from 2-0 down. Billy actually went over to Ireland after this match and watched the Germany game from the terraces, seeing his team win a famous victory 3-0.

There then followed an incredible sequence of 3-1 score lines where Manchester United were involved, five of them in fact! Four of them were victories, at home to Luton Town and Cardiff City, two away at Aston Villa and Portsmouth and one defeat away at Birmingham City. Billy was amongst the goals away at Birmingham and home against Cardiff. There was an interesting incident for the proposed match with West Bromwich Albion on the Saturday before Christmas. There was severe travel problems around Britain at the time due to petrol rationing, indeed, the proposed Christmas Day fixture at Cardiff City had been re arranged by both clubs because of what would have been impossible travel arrangements but the West Bromwich team were stuck in terrible delays on the railways and only arrived at Old Trafford by 4pm for an original 2.15pm kick off. The game had long been called off by their arrival, with to compound matters, thick fog over the stadium which would have called the match off anyhow!

As 1957 dawned, United nearly had a sixth consecutive 3-1 match but the defence held firm as they beat Chelsea 3-0 at Old Trafford with Billy again amongst the goals. Billy scored when a David Pegg corner was knocked back to him and he hammered the ball home. He was reported as saying,' I hit that ball with just about every ounce of strength I could muster. The timing was just right and it flew into the net from about twenty yards out' It was no mean feat beating Reg Matthews in the Chelsea goal, a player who had just cost the London side a then record fee for a goalkeeper of £22,000. It also meant that after twenty four league matches, Billy was top scorer with sixteen goals.

Manchester United had two very important cup ties of different stature in the month of January 1957. Firstly, they were away at Third Division North Hartlepool United in the FA Cup, with a week or so later away in Northern Spain to play Athletic Bilbao in the quarter final first leg of the European Cup. Billy Whelan was to play vital parts in both matches. Hartlepool had their record crowd of 17,000 on a very wet day which, of course, made for a mud sapping experience on a very heavy pitch. Showing the difference in class though, United got an early goal from Billy and actually were 3-0 up just before half time when Hartlepool pulled one back. By half way through the second half Hartlepool had drawn level, and even threatened the shock of all shocks when, with less than ten minutes left, Billy Whelan settled the tie. He ploughed his way through the clinging mud to score a fine goal which broke the hearts of the North East fans who had seen their lowly side draw level with the English champions. On the coach journey home, United captain Roger Byrne showed his man management skills to the full as he sat with Billy on the journey as he was suffering from a real attack of travel sickness, settling his discomfort by his constant chat and encouragement.

Another North East side, Newcastle United were involved in a seven goal thriller with Manchester United at Old Trafford the week after as the league fixtures returned,

only this time the ratio was 6-1 to Manchester United as they stayed firmly at the top of the table. Billy was again a two goal scorer as the team set off to Spain for their European Cup tie with Bilbao, the first of what would be four matches played away consecutively, Bilbao, Sheffield Wednesday and Manchester City in the league and Wrexham in the FA Cup. Sunny Spain first though!

Wednesday 16th January 1957
ATHLETIC BILBAO v MANCHESTER UNITED
European Cup 1st Leg

Bilbao is situated in Northern Spain, its people are intensely proud of their Basque heritage which was particularly shown in the Spanish Civil War of 1936-1939. The local football club, Athletic Bilbao, is founded on its policy of playing local Basque people which gives it such a strong feeling of togetherness.

Their stadium, the San Mames, is named after a Christian thrown by the Romans to the lions who refused to eat him. He was, therefore, made a saint with the ground nicknamed the 'Football Cathedral'. It was into this intense atmosphere, with 45,000 Basques baying for blood, which Matt Busby's young side entered the fray in January 1957 to play their quarter final 1st leg tie of the European Cup. Both Bilbao and

Manchester United had won their national championships of 1956, but Spain had two teams in this season's European Cup as Real Madrid, winners of the inaugural European Cup in 1956 were also in the competition, and indeed, also in the quarter finals.

United were in the blue shirt strip they had worn to win the FA Cup back in 1948 as Athletic Bilbao was in their red and white stripes, as they took the field in atrocious conditions. Sunny Spain? Well, the San Mames stadium was nearly unplayable as the two teams entered the field of play. Obviously, the further you go in a competition the harder it gets and this was certainly quickly evident to United as the home side took the lead within two minutes. The goal was scored by inside forward Uribe and when he added a second and then Bilbao scored a third before half time, Manchester United's excursions in Europe looked like they would be coming to an end.

Despite having had chances in that first half, United had contrived to miss them all and It was with real relief when Tommy Taylor scored early in the second half. When inside forward Dennis Viollet then made it 3-2, United's hopes were back on track, until this fine Spanish side moved up a gear and scored twice more themselves to make it 5-2, and surely putting Manchester United out of the European Cup. Then the greatest goal of the match re lit hope to United hearts. Picture the scene. The Spanish side coasting on the pitch, their fanatical fans making mayhem off it, only minutes to go in the match, when somehow Billy Whelan, Manchester United's Irish inside forward, picked the ball up just inside the Bilbao half forcing his slight frame through the mud, He beat one man, then another, where he was getting his strength from nobody knew. Matt Busby was off his seat imploring Billy to pass the ball, but finally, keeping his composure, Billy put the ball past Bilbao goalkeeper Carmelo to give Manchester United real hope of a comeback in the second leg. The quiet man of Manchester United had made a big noise at a vital time in Europe for the club.

In later years, Ryan Giggs winner in the 1999 FA Cup Semi Final replay against Arsenal at Villa Park brought back memories of Billy's wonder goal in Bilbao. Of all the many goals Billy Whelan netted for Manchester United few would have been as vital as this one making the final score 5-3 but a second leg to come in Manchester.

The day after this epic match, the Northern Spain city of Bilbao could not have looked bleaker as the Manchester United's players arrived at the airport, with their plane covered in snow with engineers desperately trying get it serviceable. The players offered to help and indeed, spent four hours using brushes to free their aircraft of snow and ice, with a real doubt that they would be able to get back that day. After even more delays, there was a sudden break in the weather and it was decided to attempt a take off. The plane moved down the runway out towards the sea and finally climbed enough to fly away. Johnny Berry was sat by a window and was quoted as saying, 'That was a close thing' Twelve months later a similar attempt was to prove crucially disastrous. This worry about transport to and from European trips was another problem for the club as they knew if they had issues in making the Saturday league fixture against Sheffield Wednesday at Hillsborough it would give real power to the Football League who had been so ferocious in their opposition to Manchester United entering the European Cup in the first place. In the event, the club were able to take off from Bilbao late on the Thursday afternoon, with as they stopped off in Jersey to refuel, the sun was breaking through. The exertions though did have an effect as Sheffield Wednesday beat the league leaders 2-1 on the Saturday. Perhaps that was an opportunity for Matt Busby to have rotated his squad, but those days' players just played and played unless badly injured or on International duty.

The defeat at Sheffield proved to be a mere blip as Manchester United continued there march towards retaining the League Championship, along with going for the FA Cup and European Cup. A visit to North Wales to play Third Division North Wrexham was expected to be a troublesome tie, but thanks to an early goal from Billy, United cruised into the Fifth Round virtue of a 5-0 victory, Billy adding a second early in the second half. United then had to play two matches in four days at the home of Manchester City, one in the league and then against Bilbao. Billy was in the goals against City as both Manchester teams went hard at each other with United coming out top 4-2.This set the scene for the second leg European Cup tie with champions of Spain Bilbao.

A night which Manchester will never forget football wise, saw a packed out Maine Road give fantastic support to United which was surely worth a goal. That did not come until just before half time when Dennis Viollet scored as the crowd went wild, and Bilbao knew that third goal Billy had scored on their pitch was now going to be decisive. Into the second half, United were denied twice by offside decisions as they thought they had scored the equalising goal in the tie, one of them from Billy. Tommy Taylor finally got a goal that stood and levelled the tie at 5-5. Away goals did not count in the competition then, so with a third match looming in Paris, it was with great relief, noise and emotion, that Johnny Berry slotted home United's third goal with five minutes left. Manchester United had done the impossible, beating the champions of Spain by three clear goals and were in the semi finals of the European Cup. It would bring a return to that country for United, and a tie with the European Cup holders Real Madrid.

The matches just came thick and fast for United with a visit from Arsenal to another full house Old Trafford, which meant over 190,000 fans had watched Manchester United in one week with this and the league game and European Cup tie at Maine Road. Arsenal was still a name people looked to as being a class club, going back through their marvellous history. Well, this Manchester United was making their own history and an emphatic 6-2 victory against a side who were third in the table, emphasised their brilliance. A name as a future signing of Manchester United, David Herd, actually opened the scoring for Arsenal after only five minutes but all five forwards of United that day, Berry, Whelan, Taylor, Viollet and Pegg showed their individual and collective brilliance as United scored six goals with only another Herd goal in reply. The equaliser came from a cracking shot from Billy which threatened to take the cross bar off before it flew into the net. Billy used all his skill and improvisation as he laid on a goal for Duncan Edwards before he himself scored a second. Johnny Berry with two and a Tommy Taylor goal confirmed this brilliant 6-2 score line which showed not just Britain, but all of Europe this was going to be a team to beat. These two more goals from Billy meant he had scored thirteen in his last twelve matches covering all three competitions Manchester United were fighting for.

Having scored all those goals in the last twelve matches, showing the vagaries of football, Billy then went twelve matches without scoring! He was involved though in some historic Manchester United matches in this goalless run, games which saw the club reach the Final of the FA Cup, see the switching on of the Old Trafford floodlights and play the first leg of the semi final of the European Cup before a record crowd in Madrid for the competition, which still stands nearly sixty years on.

Everton were beaten 1-0 in the Fifth Round of the FA Cup at Old Trafford, but there followed two surprise defeats at home, both by 2-0 to Blackpool and Bolton Wanderers. The Bolton match saw finally the switch on of the Old Trafford lights with United playing in an all red kit. Some of Billy's play though was top class, showing he could play outside the penalty area as well as scoring goals. His shot at Bournemouth in the sixth round of the FA Cup was goal bound until a defender punched it out, with Johnny Berry scoring the winning goal from the resultant penalty. United had played with ten men for a long while in this match as Mark Jones suffered a bad knee injury, but Billy's versatility enabled him to slot into different roles as required. This put the side into the Semi Final of the FA Cup and a chance for Manchester United to get to a Wembley Final for the first time in nine years. Birmingham City provided the opposition at Sheffield Wednesday's Hillsborough stadium and United quickly stamped their authority on the match and cruised into the final 2-0.

Despite those couple of home defeats, United still comfortably lead the league table and when nearest challengers Tottenham Hotspur were held to a draw at Old Trafford it seemed the title was in the bag. This enabled the team to concentrate on the first leg tie away at holders Real Madrid in the European Cup. A massive crowd of well over 120,000, even credited at 135,000 in some periodicals, saw the young players of Manchester United pitted against the might of European football in Real Madrid. On one hand an experienced, worldly wise side against a still emerging young team who had the world at their feet. Madrid were not afraid of bending the rules if they could get away with it, indeed, as United held them into the second half at 0-0, Billy was amongst those United players who fell foul of some dubious tactics, Billy getting belted in the stomach in an off the ball incident and Jackie Blanchflower being badly done by a Di Stefano tackle. When Madrid went 2-0 up however around the seventy minute mark it looked as though their tactics, allied of course to their skill, would be too much for United. Billy brought hope, however, when he beat a couple of players before providing the type of cross which that brilliant centre forward Tommy Taylor just loved and he duly headed home. Sadly, a third Madrid goal just before the end left United with another two goal deficit to overturn, although this time it would be at Old Trafford as that famous stadium prepared for its first ever European tie under floodlights.

Before all this, Manchester United wrapped up their second consecutive League Championship over Easter with Billy having a memorable part to play in the triumph with a hat trick at Burnley to end his goal drought. In what must have been a memorable trip for Billy's youngest brother, John, who was over in England with his school for an Easter trip. On Good Friday, they got an invite to Turf Moor, home of Burnley, to witness the vital league match as Manchester United closed in on those last few points needed to secure the title. Billy arranged to meet John and his mates outside the players entrance, giving them their tickets, so you can imagine how proud John would have been as his elder brother promptly scored a hat trick as United won 3-1. John and his mates were disappointed that their Easter trip took them over to watch another match the following day, Easter Saturday, and not to Old Trafford. They were even more disappointed when they heard Billy had been in the goals again, this time scoring two as United beat Sunderland 4-0 to confirm their second league title in two seasons.

Billy's goals over Easter took his total to thirty in Cup and League, with another three scored in the European Cup. These made him the highest goal scorer in a season ever for Manchester United as Jack Rowley had held that previously with thirty goals in a season. Incredibly, he would only hold the record for a matter of two weeks as Tommy Taylor finished the whole season with thirty four goals in all three competitions Manchester United competed. Either way, it proved what a magnificent footballer and goal scorer Billy Whelan, the young man from Dublin was.

With the title assured it was full concentration on the second leg of the European Cup semi final against Real Madrid, and an FA Cup Final against Aston Villa at Wembley Stadium to look forward to. The question whether or not United could again overturn a two goal deficit against a top Spanish side was on everybody's lips as Real Madrid arrived at Old Trafford for a Thursday night show down. Madrid were a class act however, and they quickly put this tie out of United's reach with goals from Rial and Kopa. What was evident though, was that this Manchester United side were themselves a class act and they fought back in the second half to equalise on the night with goals from Taylor and Charlton.

May 1957, Two Visits To Wembley, A Glorious Day In Dublin And Back On Tour
So, the treble had gone but most people in the country, certainly in Manchester, were convinced that Manchester United were going to be the first side to win the double of League and FA Cup this century as they took the field against Aston Villa at Wembley Stadium. Manager Matt Busby was one of those people convinced of what was a mere ninety minutes away. In later life he told me that his only doubt was if somebody was unfit on the morning of the match. They were all fine, what Matt, and nobody knew, was that after a mere six minutes goalkeeper Ray Wood would be flattened by a wild challenge from Aston Villa's outside left Peter McParland which necessitated him being taken off and centre half Jackie Blanchflower having to go in goal. The reorganisation of the team, now with only ten men, involved Billy Whelan being deployed in a much deeper role, but how well he responded. Indeed, many thought he was Manchester United's Man of the Match as they valiantly fought off Villa, only to go under to a couple of second half goals, ironically scored by McParland, and despite a late Tommy Taylor goal, Aston Villa won the cup 2-1.

Billy Whelan though, had no chance to take in what a season it had been for him and the side as just four days after the final, he was back at the twin towers to play for his country against England in the first leg of their World Cup qualifier. He was not alone mind you with Manchester United links, as in opposition to him that day were colleagues Roger Byrne, Duncan Edwards and Tommy Taylor. The crowd incidentally was 52,000, nearly half the number that had watched the FA Cup Final the previous Saturday, but Tommy Taylor certainly did not let that defeat upset him too much as he scored a first half hat trick, which with another goal from Bristol City's John Atyeo made it a 4-0 half time score line, and a difficult break for the Irish lads. Two Manchester United captain's, one before Billy's time and one after, played an important role in that half time interval. Johnny Carey was actually the Republic Manager that day whilst Noel Cantwell was playing for the Irish side on the day alongside Billy Whelan. Noel remembered it very well.

"I hardly dared going into the dressing rooms as we were all playing badly and some of the lads were having a terrible time. I thought Johnny Carey might blow his top, but he stood just at the door, smiling as we trooped in and said"

"Now let us see what we can do about all this"

Noel then explained how Carey just explained calmly, never losing his head, what he thought had gone wrong, having words with all those who were particularly overawed, simply encouraging them to do more. The Republic actually went out and pulled a goal back and then Billy hit a great shot against the bar. Atyeo then scored a fifth for England, but the Irish lads had held their heads high in the second half. Noel Cantwell also recalled another side of Billy Whelan, although he was a quiet man he knew how to use an impish sense of humour as Noel recalled;

"I recall one evening in our hotel at Weybridge, when we were getting ready to play this match at Wembley Stadium. While the entire team hung around the telephone in one room, convulsed in laughter, Billy rang our trainer in his room a few yards down the corridor, pretending to be a reporter from a well known national newspaper asking for an interview. The trainer, Shamrock Rovers Billy Lord, agreed, and whilst we listened in raptures, Billy Whelan's drawling voice wormed the entire life story out of Bill Lord, not sparing a detail. We never let on, and Billy Lord was still wondering days after what became of his article, and fee!"

The second half display at Wembley Stadium must have given great confidence for the return, which followed a mere eleven days later at Dalymount Park Dublin. That stadium was only a mile from Billy's home and he was desperate to put on a show. Inside three minutes he sent the packed out 45,000 crowd wild as he beat a couple of England players, one of whom was his club mate Duncan Edwards, before crossing for Alf Ringstead to head home. Noel Cantwell recalled that Billy actually nutmegged Duncan Edwards a couple of times and big Dunc was not impressed! Ireland played magnificently throughout the match against an England side which now included four Manchester United team mates of Billy, as David Pegg had come into the England side for Stanley Matthews. Sadly, for the men in green, with the clock ticking towards ninety minutes, Tom Finney beat a couple of men before crossing for John Atyeo to head home and equalise. The draw was enough for England to go through to Sweden for the 1958 World Cup Finals.

To complete this month of May 1957, Billy was off to Scandinavia to play in a couple of post season friendlies for Manchester United in Denmark, with two of the England players, Tommy Taylor and Roger Byrne this time on his side. Indeed, it was Taylor's two goals which helped United win the first match 3-2, although it was Billy laying them on for him. The second match against Staevnet saw Billy end this memorable season for him and Manchester United in fine style. He scored a hat trick to ease United to another victory, this time 4-3.

A season which saw Billy Whelan win another League Championship medal, a Charity Shield winners medal, a runners up medal in the FA Cup, appear in a semi final of the European Cup against Real Madrid, who went onto win the trophy for the second successive season, play a further three times for his country and score an incredible thirty three goals in fifty three appearances for Manchester United, ended with the football world at his feet it seemed...

CHAPTER SIX
1957/58 Part One

August To October 1957, Still At The Top With Manchester United

Billy Whelan had integrated himself into Manchester now, four years on from his arrival, obviously being part of what was now also a very famous football side helped. His strong, and indeed his families strong links with the Catholic Church, also helped create this bond for Billy in Manchester. A lot of Catholic priests were regularly visitors to matches, and one in particular, Father Mulholland at St Sebastian's in Manchester formed a strong friendship with Billy.

The start of the 1957/8 season was a very different one for Manchester United in that they went on a pre-season tour as opposed to playing the usual Reds v Blues friendly match at Old Trafford. The team went to Germany to play two friendlies in Berlin and Hanover, giving them extra preparation for their second season in the European Cup. The match in Berlin was given great support by the British troops still in the city, twelve years after the end of the Second World War, as they helped swell the attendance to 60,000 in the iconic stadium built by the Hitler regime. Billy was in fine form, helping create both Dennis Viollet's goals in the first half and displaying all his skills throughout the match as United won 3-0. Travelling onto Hanover, United won again, this time 4-2 as they prepared for the opportunity to retain their League Championship for the third successive season, a feat only achieved by Huddersfield Town and Arsenal in the past.

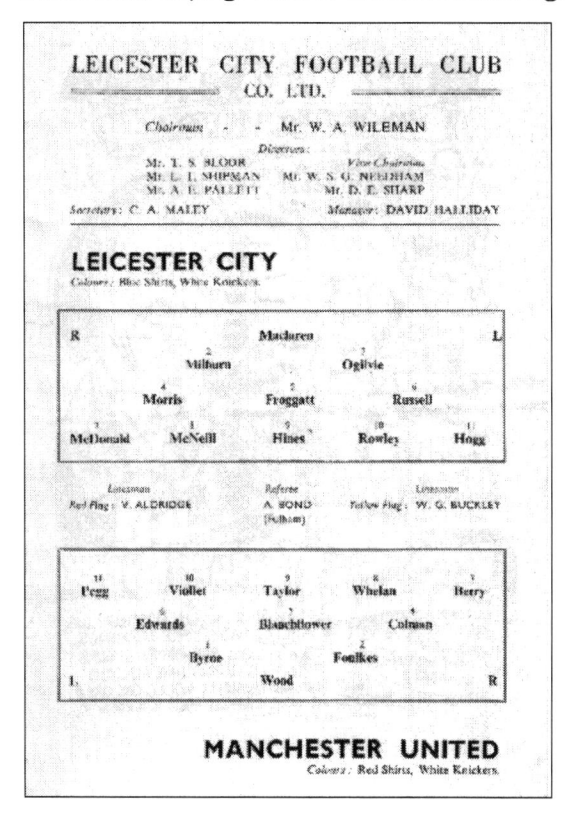

A visit to newly promoted Leicester City could have posed problems as the home side wanted to make a big impact, Billy Whelan, however, had other ideas as he scored a hat trick as United won 3-0. Alf Clarke, that doyen of Manchester United reporters via his columns in the Manchester Evening Chronicle and the United Review match programme, commented that he thought Billy would have his best ever season, commenting that his ball control is really brilliant and he had become a firm favourite for Manchester United followers. Just a point here about Alf Clarke's newspaper, in those days Manchester had two evening papers, the Chronicle and the Manchester Evening News.

After six matches Manchester United really set their stall out as the team to beat by winning five and drawing the other, scoring twenty two and conceding just five. Billy was equal top scorer with Dennis Viollet on six apiece. Three of those for Billy had, of course, come in the season opener at Leicester City, and he was on the score sheet again in the away matches at Everton, which finished 3-3 and two in the emphatic 4-1 victory at Bloomfield Road against Blackpool. In between, home victories over Everton 3-0, Manchester City 4-1 and Leeds United 5-0 had ensured Manchester United were clear at the top of the table.

When United and their followers were thinking they were on top of the world, along came two surprising defeats, 4-0 away at Bolton Wanders and even more surprising, when Blackpool came over to Old Trafford and won the return fixture 2-1. With the first round tie of this season's European Cup just days away, and from Billy Whelan's point of view a very important return to his home city of Dublin to play Shamrock Rovers, it was vital Manchester United got back on winning ways, which they did when Arsenal visited Old Trafford. The 1950's of course, did not have the massive volume of media coverage it does today for sports such as football. No mobiles, twitter, facebook, twenty four hour sports programmes on the television, not even televisions for many, with just as few telephones. Match of the Day did not start until 1964 so it is a real pleasure to see snippets of action from those times such as via You Tube. One of those snippets is from the Arsenal match in September 1957 and it shows Billy Whelan in all his glory. He is seen picking the ball up deep in the United half down by the scoreboard paddock near to the main stand, beating three men with his body swerve before playing a forty yard pass out to Johnny Berry on the right wing. He is then seen arriving at the edge of the Arsenal penalty area to hammer the bouncing ball into the back of the net as United went onto win a welcome victory by 4-2.

September 25th 1957
SHAMROCK ROVERS v MANCHESTER UNITED
European Cup 1st Leg

Manchester United's visit to Dublin to play their first leg opening fixture of the 1957/8 European Cup campaign against Shamrock Rovers, was at a very impressionable time in Irish society and for Irish sport. As we have just discussed about the lack of media information, people had not actually seen these mythical figures from across the Irish Sea in Manchester. They knew of one player though, Liam 'Billy' Whelan, one of their own from Cabra Dublin. They also knew a lot of course about what a good side their own champions the local famous Shamrock Rovers were, so to see them torn apart 6-0 opened mouths and minds. United stayed at their favourite hotel in the Republic, the International in Bray getting some sea air before they travelled into Dublin to play Shamrock, with a full house crowd of 45,000 present in Dalymount Park, a mere mile from Billy's home.

There was no floodlights at Dalymount Park in those days so it was a late tea time kick off on a very windy, even gale force, Dublin evening. United led, with the gale in their advantage, 1-0 at half time. So bad were the conditions that the half time was reduced to less than five minutes, and the quick turnaround seemed to suit Billy as he promptly scored two goals in the fifty first and fifty six minute to put United 3-0 up. This not only settled the night's match but also the overall tie and in the closing minutes United seamlessly scored three more to leave Dublin, albeit rather flatteringly, with a 6-0 victory. At least though, the Dublin crowd went away satisfied that their local lad had really come good with this magnificent Manchester United side. Billy Whelan's impact on the match and indeed his progress at Old Trafford, was perfectly summed up by that excellent journalist Frank Taylor, then of the News Chronicle.

BILLY WHELAN

"He mastered the ball, he tamed the wind which threatened to make the match a game of blow football. He ignored the frightening roar of the capacity crowd as he slipped in two magnificent goals which sank the good ship Shamrock without trace" Frank Taylor, one of a marvellous press group who relished the chance of escorting Manchester United on their travels, none more so than when the glamour of European nights came around.

On United's return to Manchester, the flu bug sweeping Britain hit Matt Busby's plans to beat Wolverhampton Wanderers in a top of the table match at Molyneux. Roger

Byrne, Eddie Colman, Dennis Viollet and Billy all had to drop out, with three or four others only just being deemed fit enough to play. Not unexpectedly, United lost 3-1 and lost ground at the top of the table. What was even sadder for Billy than missing this vital match, was that the following Wednesday he also had to miss the return match with his countrymen from Shamrock Rovers. Being 6-0 down made the tie impossible for the Irish side, but showing that fighting spirit known throughout the isles, Shamrock played magnificently, only going down on the night 3-2 with one of their goal scorers being centre forward Tommy Hamilton who, like Billy Whelan, had once crossed the Irish Sea to play for Manchester United, but in Tommy's case home sickness won the day and he returned to Dublin.

Whenever the next meeting between United and Aston Villa was going to take place after the FA Cup Final the previous May, emotions would always be high after the unsavoury incident when Peter McParland had smashed into Ray Wood's cheek bone, depriving United of a player for most of the match, and depriving them of a Cup and League double. As it was, Peter McParland missed the match due to a Northern Ireland International game, but United sent a message on how that Final might have ended if it had been Eleven v Eleven by winning 4-1. Villa, and McParland though, would be back at Old Trafford inside two weeks as the clubs would contest the Charity Shield.

Before that though, Manchester United had two very important league matches to play, with very contrasting results. First was a difficult visit to Nottingham Forest, newly promoted and, before the match, two points clear of United. A then record crowd, with hundreds over the fences virtually lining the pitch, saw United, thanks to Billy Whelan, take a fourth minute lead. The goal was drafted by left winger David Pegg and signed, sealed and delivered by Billy Whelan. Pegg dashed seventy yards down the Forest left before sending a swift low centre which Billy strode onto and crashed into the net. Although Forest equalised, a second goal for United from Viollet sealed a very important victory and seemed to have put them right back into the title race. The week after though, Manchester United suffered one of their worst defeats in the Busby Babes era...

As a young lad in the 1950's, Portsmouth were one of the famous clubs of the time. When they arrived at Old Trafford in mid October 1957 they were, however, in the throes of a decline which would take them off that famous list. Manchester United, after their fine win at Nottingham Forest were in the top three and a game in hand. A routine victory was on the cards it seemed but football is a funny old game they say and Portsmouth hammered United 3-0! It was the same day as the Wales v England International which deprived United of Byrne, Edwards and Taylor but still they surely would have enough to defeat Portsmouth? Well, such as Derek Dougan, Jimmy Dickenson and Norman Uprichard had other ideas and all played their part in this shock victory. Both Billy Whelan and Dennis Viollet chose this day to have an off day and there was no threat from United.

All the Internationals were back the following Tuesday night when United met Aston Villa at Old Trafford again, only this time in the Charity Shield. Both sides were very nearly the same line ups that had played at Wembley Stadium the previous May in the FA Cup Final, including Peter McParland in the Villa side. United were totally dominant winning 4-0 with Tommy Taylor scoring a hat trick and Billy Whelan picking up his second Charity Shield medal to add to his impressive haul.

As Manchester United reached the end of October 1957 the final opponents of the month would be a tricky away match at West Bromwich Albion, which turned out to be one of the finest matches played at the Hawthorns, remembered by any of the 50,000 crowd still alive to this day as the home side won a real thriller 4-3. Billy was back on the score sheet himself as at stages in the match United lead 1-0 and 2-1 and even at 3-2 down missed a penalty taken by Johnny Berry. In later life, the then plain Bobby Robson before his Knighthood, wrote a forward for a book I helped write on Duncan Edwards. Bobby had played his first England International on the day it turned out to be Duncan's last International when England defeated France 4-0 at Wembley Stadium. He said the West Brom v United match was the greatest game he had ever played in.

CHAPTER SEVEN
1957/58 Part Two

November 1957 To January 1958, Times They Are A Changing

As Billy Whelan and Manchester United moved into November 1957, even though they had had a sticky patch in the previous month, success in the football world, both in England and in Europe beckoned for them. They were in fourth position in the league, six points off the top but with a match in hand, with Billy top of the goal scoring chart for United with ten goals in his thirteen appearances in the league and another two in his sole European Cup appearance, with the next round of the European Cup bringing a tie against the Czechoslovakian champions, Dukla Prague.

Local Lancashire rivals Burnley were the first opposition in November, with a 1-0 victory keeping United right in as title challengers. Next a visit to the place of his Manchester United debut, Deepdale home of Preston North End, brought Bill a point saving goal for United, the third goal he had scored at the ground over the seasons for United, and moving the team up a place in the league table.

The first leg of the European Cup tie with Dukla Prague should have followed the Preston match the following Wednesday at Old Trafford, but the sudden death of the Czechoslovakian President caused the match to be cancelled until the following week. This meant United played Sheffield Wednesday at Old Trafford before, rather than after the European tie and the team kept in the mood with another victory, 2-1, with Billy continuing to create as well as score goals.

When the Dukla tie was finally able to take place, they showed a very strong defensive ability to their game rebuffing all United's attempts to open them up. Eventually, as the hour mark was passed, the door was unlocked and United scored three times to give them a strong cushion to take to Prague for the return tie. Another 2-1 victory in the league, this time away at Newcastle United, seemed to reflect that everything was back on track for Manchester United, but again, just when you think everything is looking rosy, the wheels can come off, and this time for Billy Whelan it was to have a bad ending.

I was at the Tottenham Hotspur match at Old Trafford the last day of November 1957, when similar to the earlier Portsmouth defeat, Manchester United lost a game they were expected to comfortably win. Three late changes due to injury and illness deprived the team of goalkeeper Ray Wood, winger Johnny Berry and centre forward Tommy Taylor, but Dave Gaskell, Albert Scanlon and Colin Webster seemed capable deputies, even allowing for Gaskell's youth. An early David Pegg goal seemed to reinforce this, but suddenly the wheels fell right off and Tottenham scored four goals without reply before half time, including a hat trick from their centre forward Bobby Smith who totally over powered United centre half Jackie Blanchflower. Whatever Matt Busby said at half time worked as United turned in a fantastic second half display with Billy scoring their second goal and then making another for David Pegg, but they could not pull the equaliser back and went down 3-4. This tragically would turn out to be Billy Whelan's last senior goal for Manchester United...

This was not the great boost to fly to Prague for the 2nd leg European Cup tie against Dukla, although of course, United had a 3-0 cushion. The home side gave United some problems but despite losing by one goal to nil, it was a happy Manchester United who flew back to England and a important match at Birmingham City. As with the previous league match with Tottenham, goals were aplenty, this time the match ending in a 3-3 draw.

December 1957 was turning out to be a troubled month for Manchester United, and matters did not improve when Chelsea followed their London neighbours Tottenham Hotspur by winning at Old Trafford. That victory by Tottenham had been the first defeat to a London club at Old Trafford for Manchester United since 1938, Chelsea's victory proved London buses do turn up in two's! United fielded their first choice side, a side of; Wood, Foulkes, Byrne, Colman, Jones, Edwards, Berry, Whelan, Taylor, Viollet and Pegg that had become synonymous with all the success achieved under the banner of the Busby Babes (Billy Whelan the only non Englishman by the way). This game was to be the last time it would ever appear together again...

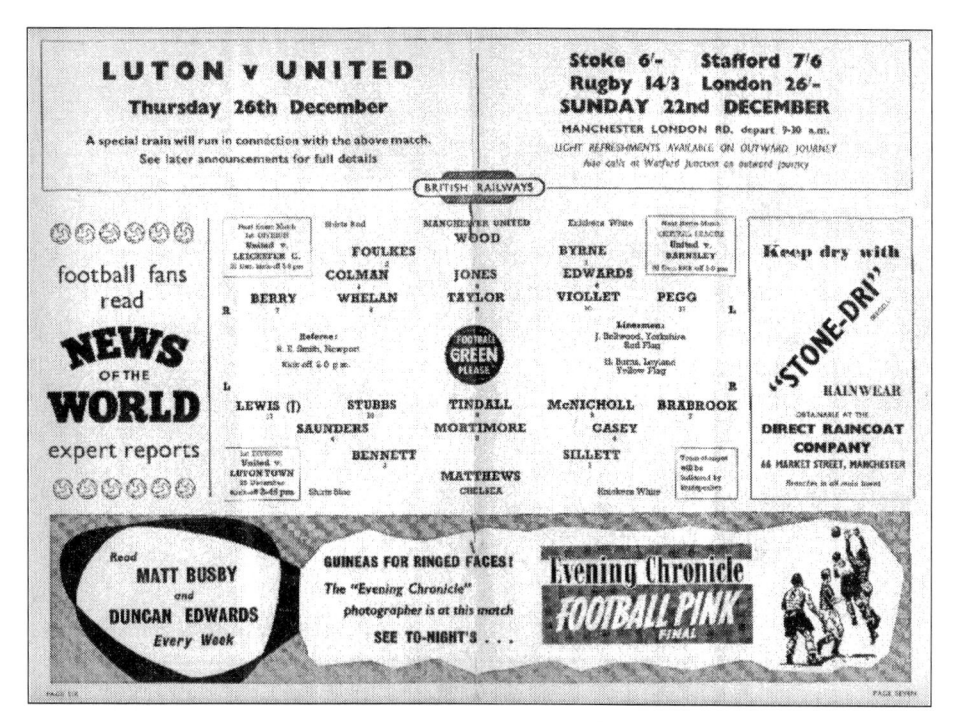

Chelsea actually were fortunate to win as United dominated the game and it was with only five minutes to go when the killer goal was scored. The media frenzy of today was not around in the late 1950's but still, Matt Busby was being asked what had gone wrong with his famous side but when he acted it surprised people greatly. First he went out and broke the record fee for a goalkeeper by signing Doncaster Rovers and Northern Ireland's Harry Gregg, a man who had almost single handed defied England in a recent Wembley International when the Irish won 3-2, but his next move really did surprise most Manchester United fans. For the match at Old Trafford against Leicester City on the Saturday before Christmas 1957, Matt dropped three forwards in wingers Johnny Berry and David Pegg AND the brilliant Irish inside forward Billy Whelan who was still equal leading goal scorer at the time with twelve in twenty matches.

Leicester, of course, were the side Billy had scored a hat trick against on the opening day of the season, but it was his replacement, Bobby Charlton, who was on the score sheet, partnering Kenny Morgans on his debut and with Albert Scanlon coming in for David Pegg. United run out comfortable winners 4-0, on the day Harry Gregg made his Manchester United debut and Billy Whelan would no longer be a Manchester United first time player.

From this Leicester match played on 21st December 1957, until Saturday 1st February 1958, Billy Whelan would be involved in seven Manchester United Central League (reserve) fixtures. Let us look at how they padded out alongside how the first team did in the same period. On the day United beat Leicester, Billy, along with such as Ray Wood, Geoff Bent, Jackie Blanchflower, Wilf McGuinness, Johnny Berry, Colin

Webster and David Pegg formed a marvellously talented reserve side which, as would be expected, comfortably accounted for Blackburn Rovers at Ewood Park by 4-1.

When Luton Town visited Old Trafford for Manchester United's last ever Christmas Day fixture, I was at the game with my late father, and Billy would have been in the stands also as the reserve side had their fixture with Barnsley moved back to 4th January. United beat Luton Town 3-0 to help this young man celebrate Christmas even more. When the first team travelled to Luton for their return, which ended 2-2, Barnsley reserves came to Old Trafford for the Boxing Day match. Billy got on the score sheet, and with David Pegg getting a couple one would have thought that United would have gone onto a comfortable victory. Barnsley, however, had different ideas and managed to get a 3-3 draw out of the match, although that still left Manchester United reserves clear at the top of the league. The last game of the 1957 season was the Manchester 'Derby' with the first team playing over at Maine Road in front of a 70,000 crowd and featuring in an absorbing 2-2 draw. Over at Old Trafford, Billy was in fine form as he helped the reserves get over their Boxing Day set back by winning comprehensively 4-0.

What would 1958 bring for Manchester United and Billy Whelan in particular? The team were in a decent position in the league, although off top spot behind a strong Wolverhampton Wanderers side, they were due to play Third Division North Workington in the FA Cup 3rd round tie away, whilst the next round of the European Cup offered another trip behind the Iron Curtain to play Red Star Belgrade of Yugoslavia. Billy Whelan knew he had a fight on his hands to get back into the side, as Bobby Charlton was going to be a formidable obstacle to replace, but Billy himself was one of the finest inside forwards in Britain, along with all the European footballing world being aware of him. 1958 promised a whole new chapter for both...

Saturday the 4th January 1958 saw Manchester United have three sides playing important matches. The first team were away at Third Division North Workington in the FA Cup 3rd round, the reserves, with Billy amongst them, were away at Barnsley hoping to hold onto their top spot in the Central League, whilst the FA Youth side were at home to Newcastle United. Two of the sides progressed, the first team overcoming a shock half time deficit to win 3-1 thanks to a Dennis Viollet hat trick, the youths winning 8-0 at Old Trafford before a crowd of nearly 20,000, but the reserves suffered an embarrassing defeat at Barnsley. Indeed, at half time it was 5-1 to the home side so I suppose the second half did show a recovery, but even so, 6-5 that was not the sort of score line expected when you consider the calibre of player Manchester United had out, including Billy Whelan.

A couple of days later, Billy joined his team mates, Tommy Taylor, David Pegg and Bobby Charlton at the wedding of Bobby's big brother Jack at Bramley, a suburb of Leeds. Bobby, of course, was the best man, but nobody could have imagined that a mere month later, three of the guests would not be alive...

Leeds United would figure again for those players who attended Jack Charlton's wedding five days later as Manchester United travelled to Elland Road for a league game and Leeds came to Old Trafford for a reserve fixture. The two Charlton's were this time on opposite sides as the first team match ended 1-1 whilst the Manchester reserve side got back some face after the previous week's debacle in Barnsley, by winning 5-3 at Old Trafford. Billy Whelan had a fine match, setting up the first goal for David Pegg and then earning a penalty from which Pegg scored his second. David Pegg completed his hat trick before half time, and although Leeds came back in the second half Manchester won 5-3 to stay four points clear at the top of the Central League.

European Cup football returned on the following Tuesday night, as the famous Yugoslav side Red Star Belgrade arrived for the first leg of the quarter final tie. Billy Whelan sat out the match, although there had been a lot of talk as to whether Matt Busby would restore such as him, Berry and Pegg, but Matt kept his faith in youngsters, Charlton, Morgans and also Albert Scanlon. Manchester was a cold, foggy night with the fog causing goalkeeper Harry Gregg to misjudge a shot to give Red Star the lead. United fought back well though to win 2-1 although would that be enough to see them through in the second leg in Belgrade on 5th February?

Before that though, league and cup fixtures were needed to be played, with Bolton Wanderers arriving at Old Trafford for a first team match and Billy going over to Burnden Park for the reserve match. The first team won 7-2 against a side who often caused Manchester United problems, with Billy having a superb match over at Bolton. He scored twice in a minute in the first half, one from close range, the other a tremendous twenty five yarder which put United 2-0 up. Bolton did come back to equalise, but this match would turn out to be even more poignant as Billy Whelan would not score another goal in the colours of Manchester United...

Saturday 25th January 1958, saw Manchester United take on Second Division Ipswich Town in the FA Cup 4th round at Old Trafford. I was at the match, as Billy Whelan would have been as United reserves had no fixture that day due to it being cup day. I remember the snow being piled up around the terraces and Bobby Charlton, Billy Whelan's replacement in the first team, scoring both goals as United won 2-0. The fateful month of February 1958 lay just around the corner.

CHAPTER EIGHT
1957/58 Part Three

February 1958, Munich...

Saturday 1st February 1958

The two senior Manchester United sides played matches two hundred miles apart on this the opening day of February 1958. The first team at Highbury Stadium, then home of Arsenal, whilst back at Old Trafford, over 19,000 fans, myself included, watched a star studded reserve side play in the Central League against Wolverhampton Wanderers. The game at Highbury has gone down as one of the finest in Manchester United's long, proud history. This one also goes down as the last match on English soil that the side known as the Busby Babes would appear. The day started off on a sombre note for the club, as one of its three directors, George Whittaker, was found dead in his hotel room in London where the side had stayed for the match at Highbury. He was 82 and the team wore black arm bands in respect of his memory, a famous picture of the day shows captain Roger Byrne, sweeping out of the Highbury tunnel to lead the team onto the field, whilst another shows Duncan Edwards, on the field of play, signing an autograph just minutes from the start of the match. The game itself saw United go 3-0 up before Arsenal pulled it back level in the second half before two more goals settled the victory for United, although Arsenal did pull another goal back to leave it as a 5-4 victory.

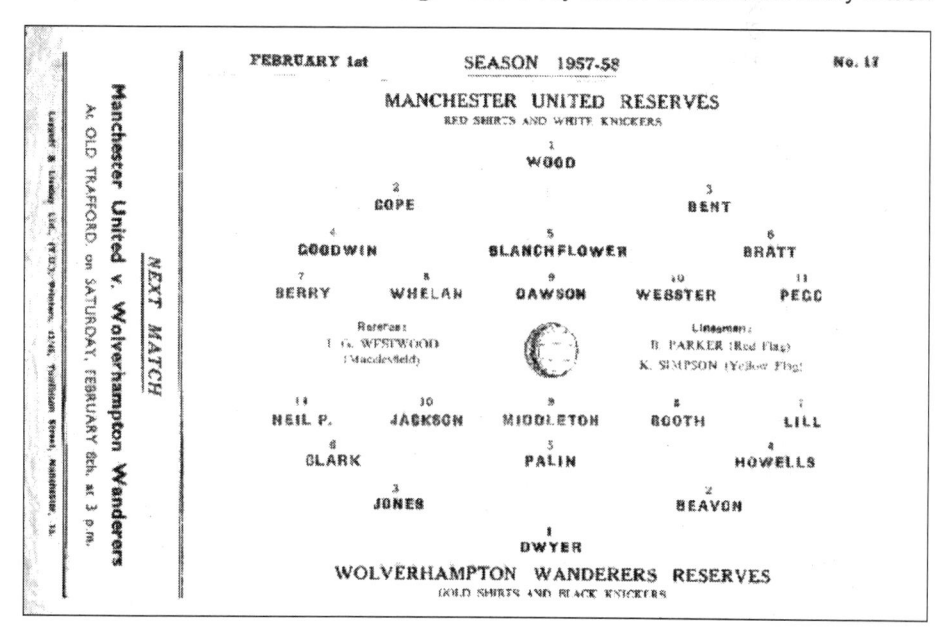

All the happenings at Highbury were transmitted back to Old Trafford for us watching fans, via the scoreboard behind the goal at the city end of the stadium. Every fifteen minutes an operator would open letter 'A' and put in the Arsenal score at the top and the United score at the bottom. You can imagine the delight to see 0-3 at half time! Meanwhile, at the reserve match at Old Trafford, Billy Whelan had created the first goal by slipping a pass through to Colin Webster to put United 1-0 up. Wolves, though, came back to lead 2-1 at half time, with one of the goals scored by a young Ron Flowers, who later in his career would become an England International. In 1958, spectators could walk around three quarters of Old Trafford, changing ends at half time for instance to be behind the goal United were attacking. The day itself was cold, foggy and I was behind the goals as Alex Dawson equalised and then David Pegg scored two penalties to put United 4-2 up, just as news came through that the first team had themselves gone 4-3 up at Highbury, eventually winning 5-4. Wolves did pull a goal back to leave the reserve match at the final whistle with a 4-3 Manchester United victory, leaving them three points clear of Wolves and with a game in hand at the top of the Central League.

What nobody knew, however, was that in the match at Old Trafford, Geoff Bent, Jackie Blanchflower, Johnny Berry, David Pegg and Billy Whelan would never kick a ball for Manchester United again, three of them, including Billy Whelan would not survive the coming week...

Sunday 2nd February 1958
Billy Whelan actually asked Matt Busby could he be excused for the trip to Belgrade the following day, as he knew he would not be in the side, was not feeling too well, and was hoping to go back to Dublin for a few days to help with arrangements for his forthcoming marriage in June. Matt, though, felt it important that the club had all its senior players in Belgrade and turned Billy's request down. Geoff Bent was to be another very unlucky man, as he was called up for the trip at the last minute due to an injury doubt over captain Roger Byrne. Whilst Geoff was to be unlucky, Ronnie Cope was to be a very lucky man, although at the time he did not feel so. He had been intending to travel as defensive cover, but Matt felt Geoff Bent would be a more natural replacement, if needed, for Roger Byrne. Neither of them would survive the trip...

Monday 3rd February 1958
The Manchester United party assembled at Old Trafford early on the Monday morning at Old Trafford to be faced by a very foggy, miserable day. Their flight to Belgrade, via Munich for a re fuel, was delayed and overall it actually took about six hours to get to their Yugoslav destination. Because of concerns about delays, particularly coming back from European adventures to make sure they were back in England for a Saturday match, Manchester United actually chartered an Elizabethan aircraft to make sure they were not tied to schedule flights.

Tuesday 4th February 1958
Whilst it was then thirteen years since the end of the Second World War, places in Eastern Europe were still suffering from shortages, although what the United team

saw when they arrived in Belgrade really shocked. All around were armed soldiers with them being on all the floors of the Metropole Hotel where the team was staying, whilst what they saw in the streets really disturbed. A few years ago, Brian Hughes MBE and I wrote the biography VIOLLET about the Manchester United great Dennis Viollet who was in the Manchester United team this trip. Dennis recalled Belgrade; "It had been snowing and the place was very sparse. People were walking around with no shoes or even having old tyres as makeshift footwear. There was no queues at shops as they were all empty of stuff. Of course, this was only a couple of years after the neighbouring Hungarian uprising and many on this trip thought if this is communism you can keep it".

Wednesday 5th February 1958
The weather had been very bad in Belgrade, cold, snow around, and there had been real doubts about the match taking place. Thankfully, the sun did break out and the pitch was thawing out as the stadium filled up for the 2.45 pm kick off. Roger Byrne was passed fit and he led the side out, with in a replica of the match at Highbury a few days previously, Manchester United flying out of the traps scoring three first half goals to virtually wrap the tie up. Red Star were, though, a really top side and they obviously had a real dressing down by their coach at half time, and with a capacity crowd backing them, came right back at United. They scored quickly in the second half, then got another goal before equalising the match on the day at 3-3 in the closing stages. Another goal would have taken the tie to a third march, as there was no extra time or penalties in those days. Luckily, United held onto that one goal advantage and gratefully got back to their dressing room having qualified for the semi final of the European Cup for the second successive year.

Awaiting them, coach and trainer Bert Whalley and Tom Curry had sorted bottles of beer and all the party, including a happy Billy Whelan of course, celebrated the victory. This continued later at a party arranged by the British Embassy in Belgrade, before pockets of the players slipped off either back to their hotel or into the city for some more celebration.

Thursday 6th February 1958
Some people were nursing hang over's as the party of players, journalists and officials made its way to Zenum airport for the return journey to Manchester, again via Munich. The journey across East Europe to Germany was a decent one but they were greeted with thick snow as they landed in Munich. The first attempt to take off after the refuel was aborted when the two pilots detected an uneven engine sound. The attempt to take off was made again but forty seconds later the same thing happened and the plane came to a halt halfway down the runway. This time the pilots decided on disembarking to ascertain the problems.

Many thought this would mean an overnight stay in Munich, but much to the surprise of most, the pilot informed that they were happy to fly on. There was no definite seating plan so the party sat where they wanted as the plane taxied and was ready for take off. The Elizabethan plane made its way down along the runway amidst a howling and whistling sound when BANG! Passengers and luggage were scattered all over the place there was an explosion and the backend of the plane broke off and burst into flames. The rest is history...

The team that was the 'Busby Babes was no more. Captain Roger Byrne, his understudy Geoff Bent who was not down to travel originally, little Eddie Colman who I had seen make his debut only two and a bit years previous at Bolton, Mark Jones the genial giant of a centre half, Tommy Taylor the greatest centre forward in the world, the flying winger David Pegg and Liam'Billy'Whelan, the graceful goal scoring inside right were all killed outright. The might of British Journalism was also wiped out. Alf Clarke, who bled the Red & White of Manchester United in his writing, Tom Jackson a fellow Manchester journalist of Clarke, and like him a contributor to the club programme the 'United Review', Frank Swift formally one of England's greatest ever goalkeepers now a News of the World journalist, Don Davies known as 'Old International', Eric Thornton of The Mail, Henry Rose of The Express, Archie Ledbrooke of The Mirror and George Follows of The Herald. Three of Manchester United's vital backroom staff in club secretary Walter Crickmer, trainer Tom Curry, and assistant coach Bert Whalley all perished. Three others on board Walter Satinoff, B.P.Miklos and W.T.Cable were amongst the twenty one people killed outright.

Fifteen days after the crash, the lad who had become a man, already amongst the greatest players in the world, and to this day counted as Manchester United's finest footballer Duncan Edwards, succumbed to his injuries. The team, the club were decimated, only the strength of assistant manager Jimmy Murphy who had missed the trip as he was leading Wales in a World Cup qualifier against Israel, held it all together in the aftermath of the Munich air disaster.

Incredibly, three months later the club competed in the FA Cup Final and played the semi final of the European Cup. That they lost was not the point, the club had started to recover, which through the next sixty years has seen them become one of the most famous and finest football clubs in the world.

Chapter Nine
Just who was Liam 'Billy' Whelan?

Liam 'Billy' Whelan
Born; 01.04.35 - Died; 06.02.58
Debut Manchester United 1st XI; 20.03.55 v Preston North End
Last Manchester United 1st XI appearance; 14.12.57 v Chelsea
Total 1st XI Appearances/Goals Manchester United;
Appearances; 98, 79 League,6 FA Cup, 11 European Cup,2 Charity Shield.
Goals; 52, 43 League, 4 FA Cup, 5 European Cup.
International Appearances; Republic of Ireland 4

Those that knew Liam 'Billy' Whelan spoke of him being a charming person, a man who always put others first, a man whose smile centred on people in his company and whose easy going personality made him people wanted around them. His strong Roman Catholic faith was never far away from him, and at this most tragic of times, it was also needed by his close knit family. A close family friend, Charlie Jackson, was one of the first people to hear about the news and he dashed round to the family home on St Attracta Road Cabra on the evening of 6th February 1958, where Billy's eldest brother, Christy, sat at home. It was ten o'clock when Manchester United assistant Manager Jimmy Murphy rang officially with the news that he had been identified as one of those who had perished in Munich. Their mother Elizabeth was totally devastated by the loss of her son, only her faith pulling her through. Only twenty two years old, due to marry his fiancée Ruby McCullagh in four months' time, a hero of Manchester United and Dublin, potentially one of the great inside forwards in football, Liam 'Billy' Whelan was dead.

His body was brought back from Germany with the roads lined with thousands of people from the airport as the cortege made its way to the family home in Cabra. The outpour of emotion could not be described. Following a service at Christ the King in Cabra he was laid to rest in Glasnevin Cemetery close to the Whelan family home. In later times the church had long talks with Christy as they realised that so many people were visiting to pay their respects that a new position was needed slightly off the road to avoid congestion. The recognition from the Irish people followed on 6th December 2006 when the railway bridge on the Faussagh Road/Dowth Avenue junction, which he used to cross going to school, also close to Home Farm F.C. in Cabra, near to the Dalymount Park stadium home to Ireland's Football, was renamed the Liam Whelan bridge in his honour by the Irish Taoiseach Bertie Ahearn. Two years later on 4th February 2008 the Irish Postal body An Port, issued a 55e stamp showing his picture to commemorate the forthcoming fiftieth anniversary of the Munich disaster.

Liam 'Billy' Whelan played ninety eight competitive matches for Manchester United in the Football League, FA Cup, FA Charity Shield and European Cup, scoring fifty two

EX-TEAM-MATES FORM GUARD OF HONOUR FOR BILLY

Former team mates from Home Farm F.C. formed a guard of honour at the funeral of Munich disaster victim Billy Whelan in Dublin to-day.

WHELAN BURIED IN DUBLIN

EVENING NEWS REPORTER

SIX more funerals of footballers and journalists killed in the Munich disaster were taking place to-day.

In Dublin Billy Whelan, Manchester United's inside-left, was buried at Christ the King Church, Cabra.

Thousands lined the streets. Wreaths came from Manchester United, the Football Association of Ireland, the English F.A., and the English League.

Among the chief mourners were his mother, two soccer playing brothers, Christy and John, three sisters, and Miss Ruby McCullough, whom he planned to marry in June.

"GG"

goals. He played four Internationals for Republic of Ireland. Whilst at times he might have looked cumbersome because of his height and slimness, he had tremendous skills, often ghosting into goal scoring positions, which would also create space for his team mates. He might have looked slow, but he was invariable the first in the mile long training runs. He was a brilliant dribbler of the ball, swaying left or right, taking players on with real confidence and skill. To sum him up, he had the control of Duncan Edwards, was a great passer of the ball like Eddie Colman and was often the leading goal scorer in one of England's greatest ever sides.

Some of the players who knew, and played alongside him at Old Trafford had the following comments to make in later years when this truly graceful, exciting, great footballer's name was in conversation.

HARRY GREGG, *former Manchester United and Northern Ireland goalkeeper;*
"People should not be deceived by the pictures of Billy as a slight rammed lad. He was a quiet charmer, but on the field he was gold plated. He seemed to ghost past players as opposed to beating them for speed. A silky, golden as I said, but over everything a genius in my opinion."

BILLY FOULKES, *former captain and right back for Manchester United and England International;*
"Billy Whelan always looked slow but if we did some mile runs he was always first! In later years he was a player we never really replaced, and we had some great players in that time"

DENNIS VIOLLET, *another former Manchester United captain, a record goal scorer and England International;*
"You see some players, a lot of centre forwards for example, who with their back to the defender, could hold them off and re distribute the ball. In Billy's case, he would just drop his shoulder and spin around and be away. He was one of the finest gentlemen I ever met"

ALBERT SCANLON, *a former Manchester United outside left;*
"Billy Whelan never realised just how good he was, in fact he seemed embarrassed at times about his own skills. He had amazing ball control, having beat you he could come back and do it again!. He had the reputation of nut megging people, I saw him do it to Duncan Edwards in training and Stanley Matthews in a match. Duncan was not a happy person when it happened to him!"

WILF McGUINNESS, *a former Manchester United player and Manager, also an England International;*
"Although Billy was a very quiet religious lad, he had a great sense of humour and would link into all the pranks that were going. He was still realising his potential, even though he had two Championship medals and a few caps for the Republic. In my opinion, he would not have only become one of Ireland's greatest ever players but one of the world's finest also. His talent was superb, ball control, eye for a goal of course, an all-round top lad!

The only journalist to survive the crash was FRANK TAYLOR, then of the News Chronicle & Daily Dispatch. Many years after the disaster, I was speaking at the famous Wombwell Cricket Society in the Barnsley area, when, suddenly this small, moustached, black haired man stood to give the vote of thanks. It was Frank Taylor. I was gob smacked, I did not know he had been in the audience, but what a pleasure, and honour to meet him. He wrote the acclaimed book of the disaster, "The Day a Team Died", a book incidentally that my wife Barbara has read three times, even though she has never read one of my twenty books! In this case she is a good judge! Let me now recall some of Frank's words about Billy Whelan. It concerns the famous goal he scored in the dying minutes of the Bilbao match which gave United a chance of getting through into the quarter final of the European Cup in 1957.

"United had given their all to get those two goals; now, in the treacly mud, they were finished. Everybody said so. They were surely out of the European Cup as Bilbao lead 5-2, nothing could save them now. But hold on, five minutes to go, and here is Billy Whelan, the quiet boy from Dublin, on the ball in his own half. When Whelan had the ball under control like that he was always liable to make it do anything but talk. That weird shuffle; the sudden quickening of speed; the rolling shoulders hunched over the ball, protecting it lovingly; the pull back with the ball; the sudden feints and stops; the crazy corkscrew turns that bore no resemblance to sleek well balanced athletic movement; but when Whelan did it on a football field it could be quite devastating. He took the ball now, lazily, and started to dribble, coaxing it along through the waves of mud, beating first one man, then another, gradually gathering pace all the time. A shrug of the shoulders; a jink and turn and a change of direction until he had wriggled his way diagonally across field from right to left, then started to come back again into the middle, leaving a trail of bewildered Bilbaoans in his wake. For more than forty yards the wandering Whelan took the ball until one wondered how he had the strength after such a hard slogging match; or whether in fact he would ever muster the strength to draw back his foot and try and shoot. Whelan ploughed on until Carmelo came out of his goal, and from a spot just inside the penalty area Whelan hit the ball hard and true into the top left hand corner of the net. A goal to remember in any conditions. In this murderous mud, a miracle goal that kept United's European Cup hopes alive. But only just".

My tribute to two great men, one, a journalist supreme, the other, a Manchester United footballer who will forever be considered one of their legends.

Liam 'Billy' Whelan, the man with two names, left this earth with such strong values, his last recorded words as the plane careered towards disaster at the end of Munich's runway were,

"If it's my time I am ready".

Printed in Great Britain
by Amazon